Words You Should Know in High School

1,000 Essential Words to Build Vocabulary, Improve Standardized Test Scores, and Write Successful Papers

Burton Jay Nadler, Jordan Nadler, and Justin Nadler

Adams Media
Avon, Massachusetts

Published by
Adams Media, an F+W Publications Company
57 Littlefield Street, Avon, MA 02322. U.S.A.
www.adamsmedia.com

ISBN: 1-59337-294-9

Printed in Canada.

J I H G F E D C B A

Library of Congress Cataloging-in-Publication Data
Nadler, Burton Jay
Words you should know in high school /
Burton Jay Nadler, Jordan Nadler, and Justin Nadler.
p.   cm.
ISBN 1-59337-294-9
1. Vocabulary. 2. High school students—Language.
I. Nadler, Jordan. II. Nadler, Justin. III. Title.
PE1449.N3345 2005
428.1—dc22   2004026396

This publication is designed to provide accurate and authoritative information with
regard to the subject matter covered. It is sold with the understanding that the publisher is not engaged in rendering legal, accounting, or other professional advice. If
legal advice or other expert assistance is required, the services of a competent professional person should be sought.

—From a *Declaration of Principles* jointly adopted by a
Committee of the American Bar Association and a
Committee of Publishers and Associations

Many of the designations used by manufacturers and sellers to distinguish their
products are claimed as trademarks. Where those designations appear in this book
and Adams Media was aware of a trademark claim, the designations have been
printed in initial capital letters.

This book is available at quantity discounts for bulk purchases.
For information, please call 1-800-872-5627.

Contents

Dedication / v

Acknowledgments / vii

Introduction / ix

More Than 1,000 Words You Should Know and Use in High School / 1

Helpful Exercises for More Word Power and Better Test Scores / 213

Appendix A:
Using Roots and Prefixes to Decipher the Words You *Don't* Know / 219

Appendix B:
Words of Wisdom from a High School Student,
a College Admissions Officer, and a College Student / 227

Dedication

To family, friends, and faculty.

This project brought together father, son, and daughter and allowed us to share words and pride in each other's efforts.

The inspiration, support, and words of encouragement of our fathers, mothers, grandfathers, grandmothers, brothers, sisters, nieces, aunts, and uncles, during good times and bad, will forever be appreciated.

Friends, who may share few words over long periods of time, still share memories and hopes for the future.

Faculty—whether called teachers, professors, or counselors—inspire us all to expand our intellectual and emotional horizons and to use the right words to express ourselves honestly and effectively.

Acknowledgments

Thank you! These two special words must be offered to Liz Runco, whose efforts made much of this book possible. Also, thanks to the authors and editors of the many, many reference books and online resources now available to inspire and support writers, students, teachers, and authors. As we developed this work, we referred to and learned much from these wonderful tools. We hope readers use them regularly and enthusiastically as well.

Introduction

Theodore Geisel, best known as Dr. Seuss, wrote *The Cat in the Hat* after an editor challenged him to write a book that would use 250 of the 400 words that beginning readers should know. Well, the good doctor came very close, using 220. Later, the publisher Bennett Cerf bet Geisel $50 that he couldn't write a book using only fifty words. He could! You know the children's favorite that resulted as *Green Eggs and Ham*. The $50 bet ultimately yielded the author thousands and thousands of dollars in royalties. Using words well does pay off!

Words You Should Know in High School has some rhyming words, should be fun and funny, and does meet a challenge, but it wasn't written to win any money (a rhyming sentence **homage** to Dr. S). It is a user-friendly reference guide written by Burton J. Nadler in collaboration with his two children, Justin and Jordan, who are in high school and college. In this book, you'll find more than 1,000 handy words and definitions that high school students of all levels should know. Each entry features a word, its definition, and an example of that word in a sentence. In much of its format, this book follows the example of two previous titles also published by Adams Media: *The Words You Should Know* by David Olsen, and *More Words You Should Know* by Michelle Bevilacqua.

A few things make this book different and just right for someone in high school. First of all, the language here is tailored for teens, and the book is intended to be informative, **pithy,** and fun to read. The varied perspectives of the **collaborators** who created it should also maximize this book's credibility and help readers relate to its honest, friendly, and confident voices. The book presents the views of Justin, a high school student who is judged every day on the words he uses, and Jordan, a college student, who can **attest** to how crucial vocabulary is when seeking admissions to college and when seeking to succeed in academics and more.

If you're reading *Words You Should Know in High School,* you are most likely a high school student interested in improving your vocabulary to get ahead. You're probably not seeking to become an **etymologist,** so your career **aspirations** haven't made you a **voracious** seeker of word knowledge. Okay, so thinking about writing and speaking is definitely not as much fun as catching a flick with friends. But words aren't all that bad. Really! And this book is definitely for you! You can use this book as a way to **accrue** a larger vocabulary, as a study aid, or as a last-minute review handbook. You can also use this book to help you write killer essays, when **cramming** for quizzes or exams, or to enhance scores on standardized tests such as the SAT.

Words You Should Know in High School can also be used to **elicit** praise from the parents of your significant other, or to wow 'em at your summer job interview. No matter what your vocabulary needs, this book can help you with the academic, social, and other **milestone** events you'll experience in the next few years.

The words contained in this book will help you no matter your grade or academic level. It will help you eliminate **procrastination,** avoid **mortification,** and maximize **inspiration!** If you don't know what any of the three **suffix**-sharing words in the previous sentence mean, you can look them up! As you might have guessed already, *suffix,* along with the other words in **bold type** in the last few paragraphs, are all among those defined later in this book. Don't worry—if you're not sure what they all mean right now, you will know soon enough.

By using this book, you are preparing to take important next steps on your path to success. The pages that follow will expand your knowledge and help you to grow and succeed. So read on, follow the advice, and you'll be in for a treat! While you may not see it now, pieces of this book will travel with you into your college years and beyond.

Now, to tell you a little more about the authors of this cool publication, here are some brief bios:

Burt Nadler has been an Assistant Dean of the College and Director of the Career Center at University of Rochester since 1998. Within these roles he has been actively involved in the university's admissions efforts and other areas of student life. He regularly reviews and edits documents that greatly impact students in their quest for success, including resumes, cover letters, and graduate school personal statements.

Justin Nadler is a member of the Pittsford Mendon (New York) High School Class of 2005. He is a proud member of the Pittsford Lacrosse Team, as a midfielder. Justin has successfully faced many academic challenges with determination, and he has used many resources including tutorial services and supplementary study guides. His academic strengths include sports marketing, art, and Spanish.

Jordan Nadler is a member of Cornell University's Class of 2005. She has studied at the University of London's School of African Studies, and she has completed the University of Dreams and the Washington Center for Internships programs. At Cornell, she is a dual major in Near Eastern studies and government who has earned dean's list recognition for all academic semesters. With her father, Burt, Jordan coauthored *The Adams College Admissions Essay Handbook,* sharing with her peers many of the lessons she has learned as a college applicant and an admissions essay writer.

More Than 1,000 Words You Should Know and Use in High School

This list of words is offered as a reference tool that can be used as a mini dictionary and as a guide to improving your vocabulary. As you first read the list, see how many of the words you already know, and also pay attention to those that seem familiar. Have you ever used any in your essays, papers, or daily conversation? Well, you should! The more you use new words, and the more comfortable you are expanding your vocabulary, the better. The other results—getting better grades, impressing teachers and adults, and achieving your goals—aren't that bad, either.

This section is designed to be easy and enjoyable to read. The list contains simple as well as sophisticated words, with definitions of their most common usages. The objective of *Words You Should Know in High School* is first to help you learn words you will probably find in your academic and practical reading and, second, to inspire you to use these words when writing and speaking. Some words are tagged with mnemonic devices, which are creative statements meant to help you remember their definitions. For words that don't have these simple, sometimes silly, always easy-to-remember memory aids, you may want to try to think of your own ways to remember the words. In many cases, we also give you words with similar spelling or pronunciation, with a clear distinction between them.

You may also want to use a highlighter as you review the list to identify new words on your list of "favorites" or those you want to use to impress friends, family, or faculty. Also, if you are working on a writing assignment for one of your classes, or on your college admissions essay, identify those words that will just plain show how smart you are.

abash (uh-BASH), verb

To make another feel ashamed, embarrassed, uncomfortable, or humiliated. To make someone feel uncomfortable, including yourself, or to cause someone to lose composure. (Hey, isn't that the definition of what people do in junior high?)

*Traditionally, high school athletes **abash** new team members; some call it rookie or freshmen hazing.*

abate (uh-BATE), verb

To put an end to, diminish, or reduce something in intensity. To lessen or weaken another thing.

*With a zit on your face, you may fear that your potential to date will rapidly **abate**.*

abdicate (AB-di-kate), verb

To formally give up a position or responsibility; commonly, refers to royalty renouncing the throne. To step down from a high government office or other powerful position. "You're abdicating your responsibilities" may be a fancy phrase you've heard from Mom, Dad, or the principal.

*King Edward VIII, as you may know, **abdicated** the throne rather than give up the woman he loved.*

aberration (a-buh-RAY-shun), noun

A departure (usually temporary) from what is normal, desirable, or expected; divergence from a moral standard; deviation from a customary, natural course of action. Also a defect in a lens or mirror that causes a distorted image. A fancy way to say *something strange.*

*Justin's one bad grade seemed to be an **aberration** given his history of strong academic performance.*

abet (uh-BET), verb

To assist someone in an activity that is probably illegal. To encourage or assist with a plan or activity, as in the case of an accomplice to a robbery. Yes, it's easier to say *help,* but it doesn't sound as impressive.

*You often hear the phrase "aid and **abet**" on crime shows like* Law and Order.

abhor (ab-HORE), verb

To find something or someone loathsome, contemptible, reprehensible, or repulsive. While it rhymes with *adore,* this word means quite the opposite.

*Many **abhor** reality shows that feature plastic surgery because they find the visual images detestable and the topic contemptible.*

abide (uh-BIDE), verb

To patiently wait or tolerate. To abide is to endure; to bear or accept a person or condition; to withstand or persevere. In the old days, it meant to live or reside in a place; one would "abide" in an "abode." While you may abide someone or something, you really don't want that person or thing by your side.

*Sitters can only **abide** the constant whining of misbehaving children for so long before they threaten to call their parents.*

abject (AB-jekt), adjective

Allowing no hope of improvement or relief. In a state of hopelessness, destitution, or resignation. Describes the most miserable kind of situation; the most wretched or degraded person or thing. Can also mean extremely humble, as in an apology or request. Rather than feeling pity, some might object to an abject thing or person.

*Many spring break partiers are not aware that in many Caribbean countries, **abject** poverty is often found side-by-side with luxury hotels, spas, and resort properties.*

abjure (ab-JOOR), verb

To renounce, repudiate, or give up one's previously held beliefs. To solemnly swear off or recant. Busted teens abjure (even if they don't know it) when they swear they'll give up their troubled ways and be good forever.

*When taking the U.S. oath of citizenship, one must **abjure** allegiance to any other nation.*

ablution (ah-BLOO-shun), noun

An act of ceremonial washing or cleansing, usually religious, as in a priest's hands during Mass. Can also refer to any cleansing, purification, or purging.

*Getting pushed into the gym pool and yelling "Holy cow, that's cold!" doesn't count as an **ablution.***

abnegate (AB-ne-gate), verb

To renounce something or deny it to yourself, in particular something considered vital or important, such as food in the case of a hunger strike. To give up, as in rights or claims.

Stephanie **abnegated** *fried food and soda before the prom, hoping to fit into her newly purchased dress.*

aboriginal (a-buh-RIDGE-ih-nul), adjective

Indigenous or native; something that existed first, or an area's first inhabitants. Used in reference to the Aborigines of Australia. The root "original" is part of this word and communicates much of the meaning of "aboriginal."

In most cases, **aboriginal** *people sadly have little or no say in issues related to their original homeland.*

abortive (uh-BOR-tive), adjective

Failing to reach completion; unsuccessful or fruitless.

Apollo 13 *was the most famous* **abortive** *mission of the U.S. space program.*

abrade (uh-BRADE), verb

To wear away, rub off, or erode through friction. To break or wear down in a spiritual sense. Over time, a wood post will abrade a braided rope.

In the past, revelations about infidelity **abraded** *voter support for candidates, but now such character traits don't seem that important.*

abrogate (A-bro-gate), verb

To formally (and with authority) repeal or cancel something, such as an agreement or a contract. To take official action leading to such an end. To abrogate a bad deal early or late is just as great.

The two business partners agreed to **abrogate** *their contract after they discovered their venture was no longer profitable.*

abscond (ab-SKOND), verb

To run away secretly, often to avoid arrest or criminal charges, and hide yourself. Absconding with funds isn't fun; it's a crime, so you'll do the time.

The plan was to rob the jewelry store, **abscond** *to a safe location, and later fence the goods.*

absolve (ab-ZOLV), verb

To publicly or formally pronounce someone guiltless and blameless. To release someone from any responsibility for an alleged misdeed or, for a priest, to forgive them of sins. When a crime is solved, some are absolved, while the guilty parties are arrested or jailed.

Over the objections of the district attorney, the judge absolved the accused of all charges.

abstemious (ab-STEE-me-us), adjective

Not overindulgent in food or drink; moderate in terms of consumption. The abstemious abstain, and as a result, weigh less.

In these days of conspicuous consumption, it is harder to find individuals following an abstemious lifestyle.

abstruse (ab-STROOSE), adjective

Obscure, complex, and difficult to comprehend. Refers to something that requires special effort to grasp. Many high school students find parents to be abstruse.

After the first few classes, Jack thought calculus was an abstruse collection of abstract ideas, and at the end of the semester, he realized his initial impressions were correct.

a capella (ah kuh-PEH-la), adjective

Without accompaniment from musical instruments, usually in reference to singing, often in a rhythmic and inventive vocal style. Don't try out to be the pianist for an a capella group, because you won't get the job.

Singing groups are so popular at that college that every weekend brings at least one a capella concert.

accede (ak-SEED), verb

To give consent or agree to something. To attain or formally accept a high position, or to be party to an international agreement or treaty.

It is the policy of the U.S. government to never accede to the demands of terrorists.

accentuate (ak-SEN-shoo-ate), verb

To make a feature of something more noticeable. To put emphasis on a syllable, word, or phrase. To strengthen or heighten the effect of something. Comedians sometimes accentuate accents to get laughs.

The architects determined that large bay windows would **accentuate** *the colonial style of the new home.*

accolade (A-keh-lade), noun

An expression of high praise and esteem. Acknowledgement, praise, and public recognition of an achievement.

Students who enroll in Ivy League schools usually have a history of **accolades** *and academic achievements.*

Where'd That Word Come From?

Accolade—In medieval times, men were knighted in a ceremony called the *accolata* (from the Latin *ac*, "at," and *collum*, "neck"), named for the hug around the neck received during the ritual, which also included a kiss and tap of a sword on the shoulder. From *accolata*, we get the English word *accolade* for an award or honor.

---

accrue (uh-CRUE), verb

To gather over a period of time; accumulate or grow. To realize an increase or accumulation by gradual means. A crew can accrue possessions in a week, or maybe two.

Money held in a bank will **accrue** *interest over time.*

acquiescence (A-kwee-ESS-unce), noun

Passive agreement without objection. Assent or compliance with another's demands. A fancy way to say, "No problem, man."

Being a physician requires complete **acquiescence** *to the intellectual and emotional demands of the career, from the first day of medical school onward.*

acrid (A-krid), adjective
Strong and bitter in smell or taste. Unpleasantly pungent to the smell or taste. Can also describe a bitter tone or harsh verbal exchange. Acid would smell acrid, and harsh words do stink.

*Her anger was released in the **acrid** remarks she hurled at her father.*

acrimonious (a-krih-MOH-nee-us), adjective
Bitter, angry, or filled with resentment. Used to describe mean-spirited or ill-natured language or exchanges that are filled with animosity. "Acrid" and "acrimonious" have the same first three letters as well as similar meanings.

***Acrimonious** marriages cause stress and anxiety for all involved and inevitably end in divorce.*

acronym (a-kroh-NIM), noun
A word that is formed from the initials or other parts of several words, such as NATO (for "North Atlantic Treaty Organization").

*GIGO is an **acronym** that computer programmers created to stand for the phrase "garbage in, garbage out."*

acrophobia (a-croh-FO-bee-a), noun
An irrational fear of high places, characterized by feelings of dread, danger, and helplessness.

*It's almost impossible to find a roofer with **acrophobia**, at least one who isn't unemployed.*

acumen (a-CUE-men), noun
Quick insight. Also, the ability to make fast, accurate evaluations or judgments about people, situations, or things.

*Laurie was said to have great business **acumen** because every venture she became involved in quickly turned a profit.*

acute (a-CUTE), adjective
Extremely serious, painful, sharp, shrewd, perceptive, or severe. Keenly perceptive, intellectual, and sensitive to details. Also used in reference to a disease that is severe and quick to crisis.

*Most teenage girls have **acute** skills when it comes to identifying a cute boy; it's like a form of radar.*

adage (A-dij), noun

A short traditional saying that expresses something accepted as a general truth. Examples of these brief, commonly accepted expressions include "A stitch in time saves nine" and "Actions speak louder than words."

*Though it is a cliché, athletes are fond of quoting the **adage**, "We'll take one game at a time."*

adamant (A-duh-munt), adjective

Very determined and not influenced by appeals to reconsider or change one's mind. Stubborn and unyielding. Most adolescents are adamant that they are right and that everyone else, particularly parents, is WRONG!

*Despite the concerns of his parents, Steve was **adamant** about not attending college after graduating from high school.*

addendum (a-DEN-duhm), noun

Something added, or a supplement to a book or magazine. If you are addin' 'em, it's an addendum.

*No matter how thorough the committee's report was, someone always wanted to suggest an **addendum**.*

adept (a-DEPT), adjective

Highly proficient, skilled, or expert.

*The league's most valuable player was **adept** at hitting home runs, particularly with men on base late in the game.*

ad hoc (ad HOK), adjective

Set up in response to a particular situation or problem; not focused on general issues. Formed for immediate or specific need. From the Latin meaning "for this purpose."

*As a response to student concerns, an **ad hoc** committee was formed to investigate the current dress code.*

ad infinitum (ad in-fi-NEYE-tum), adjective

Forever, or for so long as to seem endless. This Latin phrase translates as "to infinity." Can be used to describe some lectures given by parents or teachers.

*After reading an initial draft of the speech, the candidate's aide commented that the speech rambled on **ad infinitum**, and so it was thoroughly edited.*

adjudicate (a-DJOO-di-cate), verb
To reach a judicial decision. To use an official procedure to hear and settle a case, usually within a legal setting. A judge tried the case, so he could adjudicate.

*Those on the Supreme Court **adjudicate** only the most difficult cases and only those with constitutional implications.*

adroit (a-DROIT), adjective
Endowed with physical or mental skills. Ingenious, nimble, expert, or skillful; adept at accomplishing a goal.

*Michael Jordan, a supremely **adroit** basketball player, wasn't nearly as skilled when he played minor league baseball.*

aesthetic (ess-THE-tik), adjective
Sensitive to or appreciative of art or beauty. Relating to *aesthetics*, the branch of philosophy that examines the nature of beauty.

*The **aesthetic** qualities of the house didn't match the high price its sellers were asking, for it was rather simple and unassuming.*

affinity (uh-FI-nih-tee), noun
A natural attraction or inherent similarity between two people or things. To be similar in structure or closely connected, as with ideas or concepts.

*Dr. Seuss's **affinity** for rhyming words resulted in much happiness for several generations of children.*

aggrandize (uh-GRAN-dize), verb
To increase the size, scope, power, wealth, status, or influence of someone or something. To make someone or something appear bigger or better, often through exaggerated praise. You can aggrandize a guy's ego to a grand size.

*The boxer Muhammad Ali was known to **aggrandize** his own abilities, just before pulverizing his opponents.*

akin (uh-KIN), adjective
Related by blood. Similar or closely related to someone or something; related by common features or qualities. A "kin" is "akin" to a family member.

*Jodi's constant exaggerations were **akin** to lies, but she believed they were just embellishments.*

alacrity (uh-LA-krih-tee), noun
Promptness; eager and speedy readiness. Action characterized by speed and politeness.
*Mark's **alacrity** when a call came for help was always appreciated.*

allay (uh-LAY), verb
To calm a strong emotion like anger, fear, or suspicion. To relieve, ease, or reduce pain or painful feelings.
*The CEO met with the entire staff to **allay** their fears regarding possible lay-offs and firings.*

allude (uh-LOOD), verb
To refer to someone or something without using a name or identification, while still making clear who or what is being referenced. To make passing reference. Sometimes it's best to allude to a dude, but not use his name, for it would be crude.
*Politicians often **allude** to their "esteemed opponent," and everyone knows exactly who they mean.*

altruism (AL-troo-IH-zum), noun
Behavior or attitude that is unselfish and intended for the welfare of others. The belief that acting for the benefit of others is good.
*It is very gratifying to see that wealthy individuals can display **altruism** as well as business acumen.*

amalgamate (uh-MAL-guh-mate), verb
To combine two or more groups into a whole, or to join multiple things together to form a unified unit. In technical terms, to alloy or unite a metal with mercury.
*Anticipating that the two departments would soon **amalgamate**, the members held several strategic planning meetings.*

ambiance (AWM-bee-awnce), noun
The typical atmosphere, feeling, or mood of a place.
*The new restaurant became popular for its **ambiance** as well as for its food and drink.*

ambidextrous (am-bih-DEX-truss), adjective
Able to use the left or right hand with equal skill.

*While it appeared she was naturally **ambidextrous**, her ability to shoot jump shots with either hand came only after years of practice.*

Where'd That Word Come From?

Ambidextrous—This word combines two Latin roots: *ambi-*, meaning "both," and *dexter*, meaning "right." The word therefore implies that being ambidextrous gives you two right hands, as the right hand has long been thought to be superior to the left. You might think of this word as the complete opposite of saying someone has two left feet, an expression for clumsiness.

---

ambivalent (am-BI-vuh-lent), adjective
Uncertain, with mixed or conflicted feelings. Of two minds regarding a potential course of action.

*Although he was **ambivalent** about both candidates, when election day came Gregory made his choice and cast his ballot.*

amble (AM-bul), verb
To walk leisurely and slowly in a relaxed manner; to saunter or stroll.

*Some tourists **amble** up and down the boardwalk in Atlantic City, while others remain firmly in one seat, playing blackjack.*

ameliorate (uh-MEEL-yoh-rate), verb
To improve or upgrade. To make better or put right. When an unacceptable state of affairs is changed for the better, it is said to have been ameliorated.

*The marriage counselor's attempts to **ameliorate** conflicts between the Smiths were welcomed, but, unfortunately, they were not successful.*

amenable (uh-MEE-nuh-bul), adjective
Agreeable to suggestions; likely to cooperate; accountable for actions. Parents and teachers would like high school students to be amenable.

*Students were **amenable** to a new dress code if they were asked to give input when it was being decided.*

A

amend (uh-MEND), verb

To formally change a document in order to improve or correct. To rectify or improve upon. To alter in face of new circumstances or information. If I amend, I mend the broken and make it better.

*Representative Smith's expertise surfaced when she was asked to **amend** the appropriations bill in ways amenable to members of both parties.*

amenity (uh-ME-nih-tee), noun

A useful, attractive, or pleasant feature. A service, manner, or feature that gives pleasure or satisfaction.

*No longer satisfied with a minor **amenity** like a mint on the pillow, frequent guests at five-star hotels demand much more.*

amiable (AY-me-uh-bul), adjective

Pleasant and friendly; cordial, with a happy disposition, and easy to get along with.

*My friend Amy is able to get along with everyone because she is **amiable**.*

amorphous (uh-MOR-fuss), adjective

Without any clear shape or structure; formless. Vague or poorly defined.

*The editor found the manuscript an **amorphous** collection of ideas, scenes, and characters, and not yet a well-crafted novel.*

anachronism (a-NA-kruh-nih-zum), noun

Something out of place because it is from a different period of time. A person, idea, or action that belongs to a different time in history. Something or someone in the wrong historical or chronological setting.

*Shakespeare was famous for surprising readers and audiences with **anachronisms**, like clock chimes during the days of Julius Caesar, well before the invention of such timepieces.*

anagram (A-nuh-GRAM), noun

A word or phrase spelled from the rearranged letters of another word or phrase: "no more stars" is an anagram of *astronomers*.

***Anagrams** can be used as memory devices and can also be enjoyed as fascinating word puzzles.*

analogous (a-NA-luh-gus), adjective
Similar to another person, idea, or thing; as in ideas or concepts, possessed of similarities that would allow an analogy to be made among them. Also used to describe body parts or organs with equivalent functions.

*For athletes in sports such as water polo or gymnastics, winning an Olympic gold medal is **analogous** to winning the Super Bowl or the World Series.*

anarchy (A-nahr-key), noun
The absence of any system of government. A disordered, chaotic, and uncontrolled situation. A description of most high school boys' locker rooms and bedrooms.

*Too often, the presence of a substitute teacher leads to **anarchy** in the classroom.*

anathema (uh-NA-theh-muh), noun
Someone or something that is greatly disliked, detested, or shunned. Someone or something cursed, denounced, or excommunicated by a religious authority.

*The events of the Holocaust are **anathema** to all moral and civilized human beings.*

ancillary (ANT-sih-luhr-ee), adjective
In a position of secondary or lesser importance; subordinate. Responsible for providing support or performing support duties. My Aunt Hillary is ancillary to my mom, but I still listen to her.

*Those who serve in **ancillary** roles are often unsung heroes and deserving of more kudos than they regularly receive.*

anecdote (A-nik-dote), noun
A short personal account of an interesting incident or event. Often confused with *antidote*, which is a medical remedy.

*Steve had a gift for telling simple **anecdotes** in a way that was wildly funny.*

animosity (a-nih-MAW-sih-tee), noun
Intense hostility toward a person or thing, usually taking the form of action. A bitter dislike directed at something or someone.

*Clyde's first few months on the job were fine, but after he was transferred to a new department he came to harbor real **animosity** toward his supervisor.*

anomaly (uh-NO-muh-lee), noun
Something that deviates from the norm or from expectations; a seemingly abnormal example.

*It seems an **anomaly** when a college athlete is also recognized for academic performance.*

antebellum (an-tih-BEH-luhm), adjective
Pertaining to the period preceding a war, in particular the American Civil War. From the Latin for "before the war."

*For those once held in slavery, the **antebellum** period was not to be remembered with fond or romantic thoughts of Southern traditions.*

antecedent (AN-tih-SEE-dent), noun
The thing that happened or existed before the thing or idea in question. A preceding trend, idea, fashion, or event.

*The military Humvee all-terrain vehicle was the **antecedent** of the consumer vehicle so popular today.*

antipathy (an-TI-puh-thee), noun
Anger, hostility, and aversion directed toward a particular person or thing. The object of someone's anger, hostility, or disgust.

*His **antipathy** toward animals originated from an attack he experienced as a youth.*

antiquity (an-TI-kwih-tee), noun
Ancient history, especially ancient Greek or Roman civilization. *Antiquities* are decorative, valuable, or interesting objects that dates from ancient times.

*Museums display the treasures of **antiquity** for all to enjoy.*

antithesis (an-TI-thuh-sis), noun
The exact opposite of an idea, characteristic, or concept; a proposal that is the opposite of another idea already proposed. A word or phrase that contrasts with another to create a balanced effect. Parents are often the antithesis of cool.

*Early in the season, the young quarterback seemed the **antithesis** of an MVP because he threw so many interceptions.*

aphorism (A-fuh-rih-zum), noun
A succinct saying that expresses an opinion or a general truth. A concise summation of opinion or wisdom, such as "People who live in glass houses should not throw stones, nor should they get dressed in their living rooms."

Aphorisms may seem oversimplified to some, but when you think about it, their basic wisdom is often quite striking.

aplomb (uh-PLUM), noun
Confidence, skill, and poise in difficult or challenging situations. Remaining calm around a bomb is a sure sign of aplomb.

The entire family handled the difficult period of the memorial service and funeral with aplomb.

apocryphal (uh-PO-krih-fuhl), adjective
Probably not true, but widely believed to be so. Generally accepted or repeated as fact, though excluded from the official version of events. A story that is fabricated long after the fact is considered apocryphal. Did George Washington really have "a pocket full" after chopping down the cherry tree?

It is hard to believe that some still think that the Apollo missions, with men landing on the moon, are apocryphal.

apparition (a-puh-RIH-shen), noun
An apparently supernatural vision or being, as in a spirit or ghost. Anything that appears strange, quickly and unexpectedly, as though supernatural.

Bob's quick appearances at breakfast, as he rushed off to school, caused his parents to jokingly call him an apparition.

apprise (uh-PRISE), verb
To give notice to someone about something. To bring up to date or inform. Bill was excited when he was apprised he won a prize.

The teacher promised she would apprise all class members of their semester grades as soon as possible.

apropos (a-pruh-POE), adjective
Appropriate in a particular situation; relevant and fitting. From the French for "to the purpose."

Stan's parents did not think jeans apropos for his sister's wedding ceremony.

arbiter (AR-bih-ter), noun
Someone with the authority to settle a dispute or decide an issue. Someone with great influence over what others think, say, or do.

*If arguments between two persons cannot be resolved, an **arbiter** is sometimes called in to solve them.*

arbitrary (AR-bih-trayr-ee), adjective
Based solely on personal wishes, feelings, or perceptions, not on objective facts, reasons, or principles. Chosen or determined at random. Decided on discretion of an individual judge or court, rather than any pre-existing rule or law.

*Lynne thought her parents' rules about dating were truly **arbitrary**, for they were not like any her friends had to follow.*

ardent (AR-dent), adjective
Passionate, or full of great enthusiasm or eagerness. Emotionally intense and devoted. Hot, or glowing brightly.

*Ryan was an **ardent** supporter of his school's lacrosse team; he went to every home and away game each season.*

arduous (AR-joo-wus), adjective
Difficult, requiring continuous effort and hard work. Challenging to travel, endure, or overcome.

*Exam period was **arduous**, to say the least, even for the most dedicated students.*

ascribe (uh-SKRYBE), verb
To assign cause to a person or thing; to give responsibility to a particular person for creation of something. To identify someone or something as belonging to a particular group.

*While there was no name on the paper, the teacher was able to **ascribe** it to Mark, for his writing style was quite distinctive.*

aspersion (uh-SPUR-zhun), noun
False accusation; slander; a statement that attacks someone's character or reputation.

*Angry individuals are likely to cast **aspersions** on the targets of their hostility.*

aspiration (a-spur-AY-shun), noun
A strong desire to achieve something; a motivating goal or ambition. In a technical sense, it is the suction of fluids or gases from the body, or the drawing of matter into the lungs along with the breath.

*Most Little Leaguers have **aspirations** to become famous major league baseball stars.*

assiduous (uh-SIJ-yoo-uss), adjective
Careful and constant in terms of the attention paid to something; diligent and persistent.

*The author was **assiduous** in his efforts to complete the manuscript by the deadline.*

attest (uh-TEST), verb
To state that something exists or is true or valid, especially in a formal written statement. To make a firm assertion regarding the validity of a statement, idea, or claim.

*The prosecutor **attested** over and over that the defendant was guilty of murder.*

audacious (aw-DAY-shuss), adjective
Brazen, daring, or fearless. Bold, unrestrained, or uncompromising, especially in terms of behavior that challenges conventions.

*The **audacious** behavior of the fans almost caused the team to be penalized and have to forfeit the game.*

augment (AWG-ment), verb
To increase in growth, size, strength, loudness, or scope.

*To finish the remodeling job, the foreman said he would **augment** his crew as well as the pool of bulldozers on site.*

auspices (AWS-pih-suhs), noun
The support, encouragement, permission, or patronage of a person or organization. Not to be confused or misused with the next word, *auspicious.*

*Doctors and nurses were able to travel safely throughout the war zone under the **auspices** of the Red Cross.*

auspicious (aw-SPIH-shus), adjective
Marked by lucky signs or good omens, with the promise of success. Full of encouragement, hope, or reason for optimism, often describing the beginning of an activity or event.

*Everyone in attendance agreed that it was an **auspicious** sign that the clouds parted and the sun shone just fifteen minutes before the commencement ceremony was scheduled to begin.*

austere (aw-STEER), adjective
Self-disciplined or strict to a high degree. Somber and self-controlled, without ornamentation, self-indulgence, decoration, or luxury.

*To the surprise of many, the **austere** town librarian had bequeathed more than a million dollars to the local college.*

autonomous (aw-TAWN-uh-mus), adjective
Politically independent; self-governing, with ability to make decisions. Free from restraint, control, or regulation.

*It is thought that **autonomous** leaders have the potential to become dictators, so checks and balances were written into the Constitution.*

avant-garde (ah-vahnt GARD), adjective
Artistically innovative, experimental, or unconventional. Used to describe members of the intelligentsia (such as writers, artists, musicians, or film makers).

*It was hard for the untrained eye to determine if the art in the new museum was **avant-garde**, or just bad.*

avarice (A-vuh-riss), noun
Unreasonably strong desire for money and riches. Extreme greed.

*Some believe that **avarice** drove the recent corporate wrongdoings, which resulted in several CEOs being tried and convicted of crimes.*

avowal (uh-VOW-uhl), noun
A frank and open admission or statement. An open declaration; an unconcealed confession.

*The teachers' **avowal** of support for the students accused of cheating shocked almost everyone in the school.*

axiom (ack-SEE-um), noun
A statement or idea accepted as self-evident, requiring no proof. A basic proposition of a system that, although unproven, needs no proof, yet is used to prove other propositions. Common in scientific or mathematic theory, but used to describe any logically related series of thoughts or hypotheses.

"A straight line is the shortest distance between two points" is an **axiom** *for both mathematicians and travelers.*

baccalaureate (BA-kuh-LOR-ee-it), noun
The degree bestowed upon completion of a course of undergraduate college study (bachelor's degree). Also a farewell address to a graduating class.

I received my **baccalaureate** *in 1975 from the University of Pennsylvania, but my education truly began at commencement.*

balderdash (BALL-der-dash), noun
Senseless or nonsense talking or writing; a ridiculous, senseless, or worthless idea or suggestion.

How embarrassing for your favorite English teacher to call your essay **balderdash***!*

bandy (BAN-dee), verb
To exchange, trade, or pass words or blows. To exchange witticisms or insults.

The two brothers were known to **bandy** *both words and loving punches, but they never came to serious blows.*

baneful (BAYN-ful), adjective
Ruinous or destructive; capable of spoiling or causing utter destruction. Deadly and likely to cause ruin.

The **baneful** *influence of gangs on their young members is without question.*

bedraggled (bih-DRA-guld), adjective
Wet, dirty, unkempt, or in a general condition of disarray. She was so bedraggled she looked like she'd been dragged from bed just seconds before.

When the campers returned from three days in the woods, they were **bedraggled** *and tired, but happy.*

B

befuddle (bih-FUH-dil), verb
To confuse or perplex, mystify, or confuse. To make someone inebriated and/or unable to think clearly.

*The absent-minded professor's lectures so **befuddled** his students that they were quickly as confused as he was.*

beget (bih-GET), verb
To father, as in a child; to cause or inspire the existence of something.

*Despite the term's biblical overtones, it is correct to say that the first edition of my book **begat** the second edition.*

belated (bih-LAY-ted), adjective
Late or tardy; delayed after the specified time. Past due, often too late to be effective.

***Belated** gifts and good wishes should be graciously received and appreciated, though this is hard for some to do.*

beleaguer (bih-LEE-ger), verb
To harass someone and make them feel embattled and under pressure. To constantly confront with obstacles. To besiege (surround with an army).

*With the crowd becoming more and more unruly, the **beleaguered** umpires finally called the game.*

bellicose (BEH-lih-koce), adjective
Ready or inclined to quarrel, fight, or go to war. Warlike or hostile in manner or temperament.

*It is ominous when leaders engage their nations in **bellicose** behavior, for little good can come of such actions.*

belligerent (beh-LIH-je-rent), adjective
Ready to start a war or fight; hostile, aggressive, or pugnacious. Describes participants in a war or fight.

*Football players, especially those who play on defense, often psych themselves into a **belligerent** state prior to each game.*

bemused (bih-MYOOZD), adjective
Confused, puzzled, preoccupied, and unable to think clearly; bewildered, perplexed, or lost in reflection. You can be amused and bemused if confused.

*College students often appear **bemused** right before an exam, for they are focusing intently on their studies.*

benediction (beh-nih-DIK-shun), noun
A formal blessing or expression of good wishes. A prayer at the end of a service that asks for God's blessing.

*After the **benediction**, the congregation would meet for lunch and then work on community service projects.*

benevolent (beh-NEV-uh-lent), adjective
Kind or full of good will. Motivated by charity rather than desire to profit. From the Latin for "well wishing."

*The **benevolent** behavior of the wealthy sometimes appears insincere when it is publicized widely.*

bequeath (bih-QUEETH), verb
To leave personal property to someone after death by means of a will. To hand down something from one generation to another. Bea bequeathed her teeth after she died.

*Steve had always hoped that his grandfather would **bequeath** him his classic 1965 Mustang convertible.*

beseech (bih-SEECH), verb
To beg or ask earnestly. To entreat, implore, or request forcefully.

*The students **beseeched** the teacher to delay the quiz until the next day, as most were not prepared.*

bilk (BILK), verb
To swindle or cheat. To defraud a person or institution of funds or goods. To escape from someone or manage to lose a pursuer.

*The swindler denied that he had ever **bilked** any person of money or property.*

B

binary (BYE-neh-ree), adjective

Composed of two parts and elements; of or pertaining to two. Describes a number system that only uses the two digits zero and one.

*It is truly amazing to think that all computer software programming has evolved from a **binary** number system, giving zero and one the power to change the world.*

blasé (blah-ZAY), adjective

Not worried about something, often because of previous experience. Unimpressed; bored.

*Much to the surprise of her classmates, Cindy was **blasé** about being named to be the commencement speaker.*

Where'd That Word Come From?

Bohemian—This word was first used during the Middle Ages to mean a gypsy or vagabond. At that time, many mistakenly believed gypsy tribes came from the ancient kingdom of Bohemia (now the Czech Republic). *Bohemian* came to be synonymous with a poor writer or artist thanks to French novelist Henri Murger's stories in *Scènes de la vie de bohème* (1848), the book that inspired Puccini's opera *La Bohème*.

---

blather (BLA-ther), verb

To talk nonsense in an inane manner and at great length. To gabble or talk ridiculously. People who blabber until they lather are said to blather.

*While there are no warning labels on bottles of beer, people should be warned that overindulging in alcohol can cause one to **blather**, leading to embarrassment and the need for many apologies.*

bludgeon (BLUH-jun), verb

To beat repeatedly with a heavy object. To bully or coerce someone into doing something against their will. There's no doubt that there would be blood on Jon if he were bludgeoned.

*Forensic experts determined that the victim was **bludgeoned** with a baseball bat by someone over six feet tall and weighing about 200 pounds.*

bluster (BLUS-ter), verb
To speak loudly, arrogantly, and boisterously. To behave in a bullying way.
To blow in loud gusts, as in the wind.
*Senators filibuster while bullies **bluster**, and both verbal strategies yield little
action.*

bohemian (bo-HEE-mee-un), noun
Someone, often an artist or writer, who does not live according to conventions of society. Denotes a lifestyle free of mainstream concerns.
*According to Jim, he was a **bohemian**; according to his parents, he was just
lazy, unkempt, and lacking in ambition.*

bombast (BOM-bast), noun
Speech or writing full of long and pretentious words, usually meant to
impress others. Haughty, overblown, or pompous language. A verbal bomb
blast of long words is a bombast.
*The senatorial candidate did not instill confidence in voters, for his announcement speech seemed little more than **bombast**.*

Where'd That Word Come From?

Bombast—Originally, this word referred to a cotton used as a
padding or stuffing for clothes, derived from the word *bombyx*,
for "silkworm" or "silk," which was used for cotton as well. Just as
stuffing or padding in clothing was called bombast so, eventually,
was padded, stuffed, inflated, grandiose speech.

bona fide (BOE-nuh fyde), adjective
Authentic, actual, or genuine. Not deceptive; indisputably legitimate.
*Mr. and Mrs. Stevens bought a painting at a garage sale for $50, and they
later found it to be a **bona fide** masterpiece worth $50,000.*

boorish (BUHR-ish), adjective
Crass, insensitive, ill-mannered, and offensive. Lacking in social graces.
Boars are pigs, as are boors.
*Fraternity boys are notorious for **boorish** behavior.*

bowdlerize (BOWD-luhr-EYZE), verb

To remove parts of a work of literature considered objectionable, indecent, or offensive. Coined after Thomas Bowdler, who published an expurgated edition of Shakespeare in 1818.

*The editor **bowdlerized** the author's first draft to make the book marketable to a broader audience.*

braggadocio (bra-guh-DOA-see-oo), noun

Someone who makes overexaggerated claims or empty boasts. Also, empty boasts and swaggering self-aggrandizement. Braggarts, dolts all, are acting with braggadocio.

*Fighters who can back up their boasts are not simply full of **braggadocio**, but they are still often controversial.*

Where'd That Word Come From?

Braggadocio—In his epic poem *The Faerie Queene*, Edmund Spenser (1552–1599) gave the name Braggadochio to a loud-mouthed braggart who was revealed as a coward. The word came to refer to any braggart and finally also to mean empty or loud boasting.

brandish (BRAN-dish), verb

To wave something, especially a weapon, in a threatening or menacing way. To wave something in defiance, as a warning of potential future harm, or out of pride, as a sign of status.

*The hockey player suddenly, without warning, **brandished** his stick and skated toward the frightened crowd.*

bravado (bruh-VAH-do), noun

Real or pretended display of courage. An open display of boldness. Brave Otto proved ultimately to be most courageous, with strong bravado.

*The mayor's swaggering attitude of **bravado** was of little help when the town was finally attacked.*

brevity (BRE-vih-tee), noun

Short or brief in duration. Economical use of words in writing or speech. "Briefly" defines brevity.

Brevity, combined with the use of the very best words, is the mark of a quality essay.

brusque (BRUSK), adjective

Abrupt, blunt, short, or curt in manner or speech. Impatient (and showing it).

Her brusque actions appeared unfriendly at first, but later they were perceived as honest and sincere.

bugaboo (BU-guh-boo), noun

Something that causes fear, annoyance, trouble, worry, or dismay. An imagined threat or problem. To those with arachnophobia, a bug causes fear, and the word "boo" causes worry, so both are bugaboos.

Not swimming for an hour after eating seemed a bugaboo to him, rather than good advice.

bureaucracy (byoo-RAH-kruh-see), noun

An administrative system, especially in government, that organizes work into categories and departments. The people hired to work within such a system. An organization operated by a hierarchy of officials, often characterized by adherence to routine and lack of innovation.

The student government turned into an inefficient bureaucracy, not a group representing the interests of its constituents.

canard (kuh-NARD), noun

A deliberately false report, rumor, or fabrication intended as a joke. Also, a small projection like a wing near the nose of an airplane. It's only a silly rumor that April 1 will be named Canard Day.

Wally's story about how the dog ate his paper was clearly a canard, but the teacher took pity and accepted the excuse.

C

Where'd That Word Come From?

Canard—In French, *canard* means "duck." Its meaning of "a ridiculously false story" comes from the French expression *vendre un canard à moitié*, literally, "to sell half a duck." The expression means to make a fool out of a buyer, or anyone else, with a false story.

candor (KAN-duhr), noun
Honesty, directness, and openness. Freedom from prejudice or bias. Purity of heart; lack of malicious feelings. A lack of equivocation or doubletalk.
Politicians who speak with candor are an endangered species, one that is nearly extinct.

capitulate (kuh-PIH-chuh-late), verb
To surrender according to specific conditions. To accede to demands. To give in to an argument, request, or pressure. To capitulate early or late still means to give in to demands or debate.
Finally, after long hours of discussion, the parents' committee did capitulate and allow the Junior Prom to take place—though under very specific guidelines.

capricious (kuh-PRIH-shuss), adjective
Unpredictable, impulsive; prone to making sudden unplanned changes. That fool, who thinks he's cool, may be capricious if without thinking he jumps in the pool.
Given his capricious approach to life, it is not surprising that Andrew never settled into one field of employment.

captious (KAP-shuss), adjective
Always finding fault and making trivial and excessive criticisms. Intending to confuse someone in an argument. You've known people like this, and you just didn't have the right word to describe them—now you do!
The stereotypical, nagging mother-in-law is captious to an extreme, and teens tend to think that their parents are as well.

C

caricature (KAR-ih-kuh-chuhr), noun
A drawing, description, or other depiction that exaggerates someone's characteristics. An inappropriate and ridiculous version of an attempt to do something. It takes a character to draw a caricature, but these words are not the same.

*Political cartoons always show a candidate's **caricature**, magnifying a nose, ears, smile, or particular body or head shape.*

carte blanche (kart BLONSH), noun
Permission given to someone to do entirely as they wish. French for "blank document," signifies the freedom to write one's own ticket without restrictions. Carte Blanche was the name of an old credit card, and if someone gave you carte blanche to use it, the bill would likely be huge.

*The homeowners gave **carte blanche** to the talented interior decorator, knowing their new room would be beautiful as well as expensive.*

cartel (kar-TELL), noun
A group of companies or individuals formed to control production, competition, and prices of a certain product or good. A political alliance among parties or groups with common goals. You would care if there were a car cartel, for it would control the automobile industry.

*The oil **cartel** has for many years controlled the world's energy prices and sought to influence political developments as well.*

caste (KAST), noun
A social class whose boundaries are defined by strong hereditary and cultural ties. In some cultures, notably in India, applies to a system that divides people into classes according to the family into which they are born.

*While people in some Hindu countries are born into a certain **caste**, some believe that financial **castes** exist in all societies.*

catalyst (KA-tuhl-ist), noun
Something that increases the rate of a chemical reaction. Something or someone that makes a change happen or initiates a process or event. A person or thing that sets off new events.

*Together, alcohol and automobiles serve as **catalysts** for trouble among teenagers.*

catch-22 (KATCH twen-tee-TOO), noun

A problem whose only solution is eliminated by some characteristic of the problem itself. A situation that is illogical and self-contradictory and, often, that presents a hidden trap.

The absent-minded professor created a **catch-22** *for the teaching assistant by requiring him to be certified before taking on any students while also refusing to grant the certification until he had experience teaching students.*

Where'd That Word Come From?

Catch-22—The phrase comes from Joseph Heller's 1961 novel of the same name. In this story of American pilots in Italy during World War II, the catch was this. If you were crazy, you could get out of flying any more dangerous combat missions just by asking. However, asking not to fly any more dangerous missions showed that you were clearly sane, which meant you had to fly them.

catharsis (kuh-THAR-siss), noun

An experience or feeling of spiritual or emotional release arising from an intense experience. A release of repressed emotions that identifies and relieves related feelings and confusions. A cleansing of the mind or soul preceded by amazing insight. A fancy way to say *emotional release.*

Characters in many novels undergo a **catharsis** *after dramatic or traumatic experiences, thereby revealing much to readers.*

caustic (KOSS-tick), adjective

Corrosive or capable of burning. Acidic; able to eat away at something else. Used to describe sharp and malicious speech.

Jane's **caustic** *speech caused all the members to reexamine their support of her candidacy.*

cavalier (KA-vuh-LEER), adjective
Arrogant, with disregard or lack of respect for someone or something. Unconcerned about things considered important; nonchalant, especially in regard to serious matters. As a noun, interestingly enough, this word defines a gallant or chivalrous gentleman, especially one who is escorting a lady, although the adjective describes almost the opposite.

*The lacrosse player's **cavalier** attitude toward school may someday interfere with his dream of playing the sport in college.*

cavil (KA-vuhl), verb
To raise objections based on small and unimportant points; to find fault on trivial matters or raise petty objections. Hey, to no avail, parents who cavil will find fault, no matter how small.

*Laura **caviled** about the length of her altered skirt, but she later realized that the extra quarter-inch made no difference.*

censure (SEN-sher), noun
Severe criticism; an official show of disapproval or blame. A formal rebuke or stern condemnation. Watch out for words that are close but not at all the same: A *censor* is someone who examines, judges, and controls the content of films, plays, or writings; and a *sensor* is a device capable of detecting and responding to movement, light, or heat.

***Censure** is less severe than impeachment, but elected officials should take care to avoid both.*

cessation (seh-SAY-shun), noun
A stop, pause, interruption, or permanent discontinuation. An end to something; the reaching of a point of conclusion.
*The substitute teacher prayed for a **cessation** of the rude behavior in his classroom.*

chagrin (shuh-GRIN), noun
A feeling of humiliation due to disappointment. Humiliation, embarrassment, or disappointment; anxiety about oneself. Chagrin does not mean that "she grin"; more appropriate would be a grimace or frown.

*Much to the **chagrin** of his family and friends, Suzanne rejected Bill's proposal.*

charismatic (kare-ihz-MA-tik), adjective

Possessing great charm or influence, with a special quality of leadership, authority, confidence, and overall appeal. Also used to describe Christian sects whose practices include healing, prophecy, and speaking in tongues.

*The **charismatic** entertainer was more than a singer, actress, and model; many felt she had the potential to be an elected official.*

charlatan (SHAR-luh-tun), noun

Someone who lies, claiming a special talent, skill, or expertise. A fake or humbug. Charlie the charlatan claimed his pills made one instantly tan.

*Ultimately, the healer was proven to be a **charlatan**, but not before several people had suffered and died.*

chicanery (shi-KAN-er-ree), noun

Deception or trickery, especially that achieved by clever argument or manipulation of facts or language. What most teens try when they get caught doing something wrong, though few succeed.

The actions and oratory of Professor Harold Hill, that famous character in the musical The Music Man, *are often held up as perfect illustrations of **chicanery**.*

Where'd That Word Come From?

Chicanery—This word for trickery, especially legal dodges and quibbles, came into English through a French word with the same meaning. It seems to be derived from the Persian *chaugan*, for the crooked stick used in polo. The stick's name somehow came to mean a dispute in polo and other games, then took on the meaning of a crooked practice in those games and in general.

---

chivalrous (SHI-vuhl-russ), adjective

Honorable and courteous, as in a code of behavior followed by medieval knights. Considerate, especially toward women, the poor, or the defeated.

*Placing one's coat over a puddle for a lady was once thought **chivalrous**, but it's now more likely to be thought crazy.*

C

churlish (CHUHR-lish), adjective
Ill-bred, surly, sullen, or miserly. Unmannered; boorish and vulgar. Boy, don't we all know someone who deserves to be called this dramatic word?
Churlish behavior is never acceptable, no matter the person or the circumstances, but it is very hard to stop.

circumlocution (sir-kum-low-KYOO-shun), noun
Evasiveness in speech or writing. The use of excess language to avoid saying something directly or truthfully. Overblown and tedious writing or speech. Don't try to get around good elocution with circumlocution; speak and write directly and well.
*The use of **circumlocution** can lengthen term papers and help students meet a predetermined word count or page requirement, but it can also often lead to lower grades.*

circumvent (sir-kum-VENT), verb
To avoid rules or laws without actually breaking them. To evade by means of a gray area or loophole. To maneuver around authority.
*To **circumvent** the no-short-skirt rule, many of the girls took to wearing Daisy Duke shorts.*

clairvoyance (klare-VOY-ence), noun
The ability to see things beyond normal vision, events from the future, or those who have died. From the French for "clear sight," the ability to perceive things beyond the range of human perception.
*Clare's claims of seeing into the future, and her amazing talent for predicting outcomes, still didn't prove her **clairvoyance**.*

clandestine (klan-DESS-tin), adjective
Hidden, secret; concealed from general view or, if illegal, from authorities.
*The **clandestine** activities of spies may seem glamorous in books and movies, but to those who really work in intelligence gathering, life can be dull as well as dangerous.*

clemency (KLEH-muhn-see), noun

A show of mercy or leniency toward a wrongdoer or opponent, under appropriate circumstances.

*Jack's parents showed **clemency** and allowed him to keep his car even after his speeding conviction, inspiring him to drive more carefully.*

cogent (KOE-junt), adjective

Forceful, convincing, compelling; appealing effectively to the intellect or reason.

*Although it took a while, he eventually convinced the rest of the student council with his **cogent** arguments.*

cognition (kog-NIH-shun), noun

Mental ability; the process of acquiring knowledge through reason, intuition, or perception. Can also mean knowledge. Yes, it's just a fancy way to talk about thinking, but it's definitely an impressive word.

*The young parents were excited to see the process of **cognition** developing in their daughter, as she began to take tiny steps with her feet and giant leaps with her mind.*

cohort (KO-hort), noun

A supporter, accomplice, or associate of a particular leader to whom special treatment is given. A member of a united group or group sharing a common characteristic like age, income, or gender, especially in statistical surveys. Originally referred to one of ten divisions of a Roman legion, composed of soldiers with strong ties of comradeship.

*Stephanie and her **cohorts** on the soccer team all shared physical qualities like blonde hair, as well as mental ones, such as the drive to win.*

collaborator (kuh-LA-buh-RATE-er), noun

Someone who works with other people to achieve something. Also a person who betrays others by working with an enemy, especially an occupying army.

*The local **collaborators** who supported the German occupation of France were severely punished after the Allied victory.*

colloquy (kaw-LUH-kwee), noun
Conversation, discussion, or conference; often formal. A literary work written in the form of dialogue. The adjective *colloquial* means breezy, informal communication. A *colloquialism* is a common phrase of a conversational nature. So from noun to adjective to noun, from colloquy to colloquial to colloquialism, the definitions become less formal and more conversational.

*Our member of the House of Representatives often holds a **colloquy** for discussing specific legislation, rather than just talking about general topics.*

collusion (kuh-LOO-zhun), noun
Secret cooperation among a number of people, usually to accomplish something illegal or wrong. A conspiratorial or secret understanding to join a secret plot or plan. Not a collision, but sometimes a collusion can also yield serious results.

*We suspect **collusion** when the price of gas rises and all stations charge the same higher rates, but it may just be the power of supply and demand.*

comely (KUM-lee), adjective
Physically good-looking, pleasing, fetching, inviting, or attractive; usually referring to women.

***Comely** women hope that love is more than skin deep and that men are attracted to them for more than just their looks.*

commensurate (kuh-MENTS-rit), adjective
Properly or appropriately proportionate. Of the same size, with an equal measure or equivalent duration. You can say *equal*, but "commensurate" is a much more powerful word.

*Stewart's grades were, unfortunately, **commensurate** with the small amount of time and energy he invested in his academics.*

commiserate (kuh-MIH-zeh-rate), verb
To express sympathy or sorrow; to share in another's sorrow or disappointment.

*After the game, the first thing the team did was **commiserate** with the parents of the player who was seriously injured.*

C

compendious (kum-PEN-dee-us), adjective
Containing a wide range of information in a concise form; usually a piece of writing. Composed of all necessary or essential components, yet concise and succinct.

Words You Should Know in High School is both compendious and tremendous, or you wouldn't be reading it, would you?

complaisant (kum-PLAY-zunt), adjective
Willing to please others. Eager to make others happy; agreeable to the wishes of others. Not to be confused with *complacent*, which means "self-satisfied."

Once Principal McAdams spoke honestly with Catherine, she transformed from an oppositional brat into a complaisant achiever.

comport (kum-PORT), verb
To behave in a particular way. To agree or be consistent with something or someone. Those who comport well deport themselves with equal composure, conducting themselves in particular positive ways.

The chaperones on the trip expected everyone to comport themselves appropriately and politely.

compunction (kum-PUNK-shun), noun
Feelings of guilt, shame, and regret about doing something wrong. Remorse or uncertainty about a decision or course of action. Some punks shun others, then feel guilty and express compunction.

It is extremely sad when you see friends behaving badly yet showing no compunction.

concerted (kun-SURT-id), adjective
Planned by two or more persons working together on an action or effort. Mutual, as in actions taken toward an established goal. Also describes music written for several soloists. Much fancier way of saying *together*.

Musicians in concert act as performers concerted to achieve common creative objectives.

confabulate (kun-FA-byoo-late), verb
From the Latin for "to have a conversation with," to chat or discuss something informally. Can describe engaging, extravagant storytelling. Also, to invent and believe stories to fill mental gaps due to memory loss or dementia. The noun *confab* means a casual discussion or chat, or a gathering of people for a discussion. Talk about a fancy word for talking—confabulate takes the prize.
The two drivers stopped the flow of traffic east and west in order to confabulate about who had caused the accident.

confluence (KAHN-flu-ence), noun
A point where two or more streams flow together. A point of meeting, flowing together, or joining. To increase your word influence, use confluence when speaking or writing about meeting.
If you think about it, most of the world's religions have common origins and many points of confluence.

congenital (kun-JEH-nih-tul), adjective
Present or existing from birth, as in an unusual physical condition. Frankly, most things congenital are not very congenial.
It was very sad for John and Patricia to learn that their newborn had a congenital respiratory disorder, but they were happy to discover that it was treatable.

conjure (KON-jur), verb
To perform illusions and magic using agile hand movements. To summon or call upon, as if by supernatural means.
On the anniversary of Houdini's death, many try to conjure up the image of this famous magician who spent his life exploring the potential to communicate with the dead.

connotation (KAH-noh-TAY-shun), noun
The implied, figurative, or suggested additional meaning of a word or phrase, apart from the literal dictionary meaning. In contrast, the word *denotation* means the literal definition or meaning.
As society changes, the connotations of particular words also change, and what was once an appropriate word sometimes becomes politically incorrect.

C

consortium (kun-SOR-shee-um), noun

A group set up for a common purpose that would be beyond the capabilities of a single member. A union, partnership, or alliance. Also a legal term for the rights of married persons.

The Career and Internship Connection is a **consortium** *of about a dozen schools that participate in four off-campus recruiting events.*

consternation (kon-ster-NAY-shun), noun

Bewilderment, amazement, alarm, or dismay caused by something unexpected. Amazement or confusion at a turn of events.

Much to the **consternation** *of her parents, Stephanie, who was only eighteen, announced her engagement to a man twice her age.*

construe (kon-STROO), verb

To interpret or understand meaning of a word, gesture, or action in a particular way. To translate or analyze the grammar of a piece of text. To construe is to reach a conclusion based on review.

It is often an attorney's job to **construe** *the meaning of a contract, then share that interpretation with a client and, if needed, with a judge or jury.*

consummate (KON-suh-mate), verb

To bring something such as a business deal to a conclusion or desired end; to achieve, fulfill, complete, or finalize. Also, for a couple to make a marriage legally valid by having sexual relations.

By **consummating** *an agreement, and then signing the letter of intent, the high school All-American football player committed to attending Notre Dame.*

contemptuous (kun-TEMP-choo-wus), adjective

Feeling, expressing, or demonstrating strong dislike, disdain, or scorn for someone or something. Showing an utter lack of respect for tradition or convention.

The **contemptuous** *behavior of gang members is perhaps the most difficult issue faced in many urban areas today.*

context (kon-TEKST), noun
The words, phrases, or passages before and after a particular word or passage that help to explain its complete meaning. The circumstances or events related to an incident or action.

The context of Martin Luther King, Jr.'s, famous "I Have a Dream" speech is important for understanding the full impact this oration had on its audience.

contravene (kon-truh-VEEN), verb
To disagree with or oppose a decision or statement; go against or deny. To oppose something by action or argument. To break a rule or law. To be mean, you would contravene (or deny), often making others cry.

The decisions of coaches are rarely contravened by players.

contrivance (kun-TRY-vunce), noun
A cleverly made, unusual device or machine. A clever way to acquire something; a plot or scheme. A plan intended to deceive.

The contrivances of alchemists were machines that attempted—and failed—to turn base metals into gold.

convalescence (kon-vuh-LEH-sunce), noun
Time spent resting, recovering, and regaining one's health after an illness or medical treatment. From the Latin for "to grow stronger."

Those people who believe convalescence is done better at home don't have two-year-old twins.

convivial (kun-VIV-yul), adjective
Enjoyable because of friendliness and amicability; festive and sociable. Given to eating, drinking, and socializing.

It was very surprising that the prom was so convivial, given that adolescents can often be competitive and taunting.

convoluted (kon-vuh-LOO-tid), adjective
Too complex or intricate to understand easily. Complicated, with many twists or folds. Literally, folded into a coil or spiral. Most often used to express an extreme state of complication, intricacy, or interdependency.

Relationships can be convoluted and difficult, but they are ultimately worth the effort.

copious (KO-pee-us), adjective
Produced in large quantities; abundant.
Copious notes can be a student's best study tools.

corroborate (kuh-RAW-buh-rate), verb
To give evidence of the truth; confirm or increase in certainty. To provide testimony that supports previous theories or opinions.
Jim said his bother would **corroborate** *his story, proving he was nowhere near the scene of the crime.*

covenant (KUHV-nent), noun
A binding agreement or contract between two or more parties. In biblical terms, the promise binding the ancient Israelites to God.
Some teenagers believe promises made by parents, particularly regarding cars and curfews, should be thought of as **covenants.**

covert (KOH-vert), adjective
Secret or covered over. Concealed or surreptitious. Not intended to be known or seen.
Many **covert** *operations contributed to the success of D-day, but it took decades for anyone involved in them to be honored.*

cram (KRAM), verb
To study a subject intensively for an imminent exam. To eat food hastily and with greed. To force persons or objects into a space or container too small to comfortably fit them all.
Cramming for exams is an attempt to quickly force large quantities of facts into your memory, which, ideally, can retain all the pertinent information.

credence (KREE-dence), noun
A belief in something as factual, based on the degree that something is plausible. Faith in a thing's legitimacy.
The defendant's claims of innocence lost **credence** *as more evidence was uncovered and made public.*

C

credulous (KREH-juh-luss), adjective
Too easily convinced that something is true; given to accept or believe readily. Accepting of even outlandish assertions easily.

Credulous consumers are likely to spend thousands of dollars on diets and exercise equipment that don't really work.

culinary (KYOO-luh-ner-ee), adjective
Related to food or cooking. Commonly used to describe the type of school where chefs are trained. If you want to follow the recipe for good usage, use "culinary" rather than "cooking."

The sale of culinary books and related items increased dramatically as the popularity of television cooking shows rose.

culminate (KUL-mih-nate), verb
To reach a climax or a high point of development. To conclude or reach fulfillment; to come to a dramatic end.

To no one's surprise, Aaron's constant detentions and oppositional behavior culminated in his suspension from school.

culpable (KUL-puh-bull), adjective
Deserving blame or punishment for something wrong; accountable for errors or misdeeds.

Mr. Hartland was culpable for the errors he made while grading the English exams, so he gave the students an extra ten points on each essay.

cultural literacy (KUHLCH-rul LIH-tuh-reh-see), phrase
As conceived and defined by Professor E.D. Hirsch, Jr., "the background knowledge necessary for functional literacy and effective national communication"; from the subtitle of his book, *What Every American Needs to Know.* The information authors assume readers have at certain stages of education; the educational background necessary for effective communication of ideas.

The debate regarding cultural literacy and its part in our elementary and secondary school curricula continues to this day.

D

cumbersome (KUM-ber-sum), adjective
Awkward to carry or handle; hard to manage because of bulk, weight, size, or shape. Difficult to deal with because of length or complexity. Not a *cummerbund*—that's a pleated, often colored sash worn by men as part of formal attire.

*While desktop computers have become smaller and lighter, they are still **cumbersome** when compared to laptop models.*

cupidity (kyoo-PIH-duh-tee), noun
Greed; extreme desire for money and possessions. Cupid is a symbol of love, and cupidity is the love of money and things.

*Unrealistic **cupidity** of youth, often expressed by spoiled children, should with time be replaced by the work ethic of an adult.*

curative (KYOOR-uh-tive), adjective
Able to restore health; curing; serving to provide a remedy.

*The **curative** regimen of the spa involved diet and hot baths, as well as exercise and massage.*

cyberspace (SY-ber-spase), noun
The theoretical realm where electronic information exists or is shared. The imaginary world of virtual reality.

*It's fun to think of e-mails as floating in **cyberspace**, but they are actually a series of impulses sent and received over a variety of fiber-optic or traditional telephone lines.*

dalliance (DA-lee-unce), noun
A lighthearted undertaking; carefree, frivolous, inconsequential, or idle wasting of time. An amorous flirtation, distraction, or affair.

*Stephanie could not forgive her husband's **dalliance**, so she asked for a divorce.*

dank (DANK), adjective
Damp and chilly; unpleasantly cold and moist. Dank is damp, but not necessarily dark.

*The Williams' basement was **dank** even before the rainy winter season.*

debacle (dee-BAH-kuhl), noun

Something that becomes a disaster, defeat, or failure. Utter collapse or rout; complete, often humiliating failure.

*Wars often seem justified at first, but they tend to become **debacles** if an exit strategy is not devised and implemented.*

debilitate (dih-BIH-lih-tate), verb

To weaken or sap strength from someone or something.

*ALS, also known as Lou Gehrig's disease, **debilitates** those who suffer from it, and it is ultimately fatal.*

deciduous (dih-SIH-juh-wus), adjective

Shedding or losing foliage at the end of the growing season. Falling off or shedding at a particular time, season, or stage of growth. Not lasting; ephemeral.

*Some Native American tribes marked the change of seasons by the **deciduous** clues around them, including deer shedding antlers, leaves falling from certain trees, and feathers molting from specific birds.*

decorum (dih-COR-um), noun

Dignity or correctness that is socially expected; dignified conduct. A harmonious compatibility of elements in a piece of art or literature. Not to be confused with *décor*, which is the style of furniture and accessories in a room, house, or stage scenery.

*A visit to the Supreme Court will reveal the meaning of true **decorum**.*

decrepit (dih-KREH-pit), adjective

In very poor condition; old, overused, or not working efficiently. Lessened in strength or ability, as in old age. Used to describe a person, object, or idea that is weak and past its prime. Please don't call someone decrepit if they are just old; use this word appropriately.

*Most of the buildings in the so-called poor part of town were indeed **decrepit** and dangerous to live in.*

D

deduce (di-DOOCE), verb
To reach a logical conclusion by using what is known, without all necessary information. To infer or derive from evidence or assumption. To deduce is not to take your best guess; it means a logical leap.

*It is the job of detectives to **deduce** the circumstances of crimes, for they rarely have all the facts.*

defamation (de-fuh-MAY-shun), noun
False, baseless attack on a person's or group's reputation, name, or character. The act of defaming or bringing disgrace.

***Defamation** seems to be the purpose of many newspapers that focus on sensational stories about stars and celebrities.*

deference (DEH-fuh-rence), noun
Polite respect or submission to the judgment, opinion, or wishes of another. The act of yielding to another higher, senior, or more authoritative person.

*In **deference** to the memory of his brother, Ken did not speak about the details of his accident with anyone.*

deign (DANE), verb
To do something in a way that shows it is beneath one's dignity. To agree in a very condescending way to do something. To deign is sometimes to feign that actions are okay—or so you say.

*Please don't **deign** to support our fundraising efforts if you are truly not on board with our program.*

delectable (dih-LEK-tuh-bull), adjective
Delicious; absolutely delightful, pleasing, or attractive. From the Latin for "delightful."

*Italian and Jewish grandmas are famous for their **delectable** dishes, served with a bit of guilt on the side.*

deleterious (deh-luh-TEE-ree-us), adjective
With harmful or damaging effect on something or someone. As a legal term, communicates the assessment of harm, injury, or loss.

*It is now accepted as fact that smoking is **deleterious** to one's health as well as highly addictive, but year after year more teenagers still take it up.*

delineate (dih-LI-nee-ate), verb
To describe or explain something in detail. To outline, sketch, graph, chart, or draw something. To describe the principal points of something.

*The proctor clearly **delineated** the instructions for the essay exam, in writing and out loud.*

demure (dih-MYOOR), adjective
Modest, reserved, or shy in appearance. Used to describe sober, retiring, or sedate behavior.

***Demure** actions and attitudes are much more proper than oppositional and defiant behavior.*

denote (dih-NOTE), verb
To designate or refer to somebody or something in particular. To define something literally, as in a dictionary definition. To announce or make known. The opposite of *connote*, which means to imply or suggest something in addition to its literal meaning.

*Before the camping trip, each student received specific instructions regarding what would **denote** a rules infraction that would be punished by being sent home.*

denunciation (dih-nun-see-AY-shun), noun
Public accusation or condemnation. An accusation that someone has done a misdeed.

*It's common for litigants in a divorce to issue strong mutual **denunciations**.*

deplorable (dih-PLORE-uh-bull), adjective
Worthy of severe condemnation, censure, and denunciation. Also, wretched or grievous because of neglect, poverty, or misfortune. Deplorable is a strong word to use for those who abuse and also for the people and things that are misused.

*Some poor children live in **deplorable** conditions that diminish their potential for physical, psychological, and intellectual development.*

depravity (dih-PRA-vih-tee), noun
State of moral corruption and reprehensibility. A morally corrupt or wicked act.

*The **depravity** of those who committed the Holocaust will never be forgotten.*

D

deprecate (DEH-prih-kate), verb
To belittle or express disapproval of someone or something. To cut down verbally. Teens can deprecate those they hate, or, in humor, those they date. Most high school humor is deprecating in nature. Get it, geek?

*Verbal bullies **deprecate** others rather than using their fists, but the words hurt just the same.*

dereliction (dare-uh-LIK-shun), noun
Deliberate neglect of obligations, duty, or responsibility. The act of abandoning or deserting a building.

***Dereliction** of duty is a serious charge for those in the military.*

derision (dih-RIH-zhun), noun
Ridicule, contempt, or mockery. From the verb *deride,* meaning "to belittle something or someone." Derision deprecates, and bears emotional weight, so think about what you say before it's too late.

*Whenever these two schools compete in a sporting event, all you hear is **derision** chanted back and forth from one side to the other.*

derivation (dare-uh-VAY-shun), noun
The path of descent for something, such as a name or word, that traces back to the source. A mathematical or logical argument flowing from initial assumptions, to proofs, and then to conclusion. Not to be confused with *deviation* (a change from the norm, expected or planned), for it is a direct and clear path from a source or to a conclusion.

*Etymologists, who study the **derivation** of words, should not be confused with entomologists, who study insects, or etiologists, who study the causes or origins of disease.*

despondent (dih-SPON-dunt), adjective
Extremely unhappy, depressed, dejected, or discouraged. Despairing, with the feeling that all hope is in vain.

*Divorce respondents are often **despondent,** if depressed about the breakup or, most likely, the attorney fees.*

despotism (DESS-puh-tih-zum), noun
Authoritarian rule by a tyrant, dictator, or despot. Rule by one dominant person who exercises complete power. High school students sometimes describe principals, parents, or coaches as despots, and occasionally they are right.

*The rise of **despotism** is often linked to poverty, when the poor hope a powerful leader can bring positive change.*

dexterous (DEK-steh-russ), adjective
Easy and skilled in movement, usually in tasks completed with the hands. The word's root (like that of *ambidextrous*) is in the Latin for "right," because most people are more skillful with this hand.

*The director was looking for a **dexterous** actor who could succeed both in doing stunts and in playing the dramatic role.*

diatribe (DIE-uh-tribe), noun
A bitter verbal or written attack; a denunciation. Also, a pointed and abusive critique.

*Angry at being caught cheating, the student launched a profanity-laced **diatribe** on the test proctor.*

dichotomy (die-KAH-tuh-mee), noun
Two parts, ideas, or concepts that differ from, contradict, or perfectly complement each other. Contrasting halves, pairs, or sets. A division of mutually exclusive ideas or groups.

*The **dichotomy** of good and evil is a theme in almost all classic novels read in high school.*

didactic (die-DAK-tik), adjective
Focused on communicating a moral, political, or educational message. Presenting a clear vision of right and wrong; projecting morality. Not to be confused with *eclectic*, which means composed of elements from varied sources, or *dialectic*, which is the tension between conflicting elements, forces, or ideas.

*Some authors and lecturers are subtly **didactic**, while others are more obvious and preachy.*

D

diffident (DIH-fuh-dent), adjective
Lacking self-confidence. Shy, unassertive, or with a low sense of self-worth. Reserved or restrained in the way one behaves. Don't confuse with *defendant*, which is a person answering criminal charges, or *dissident*, a person who disagrees with an established political or religious authority.

Diffident individuals don't belong in sales positions, which require assertiveness and risk-taking.

diminutive (dih-MIH-nyoo-tiv), adjective
Very small, or smaller than usual. This idea is often communicated by attaching a suffix to the noun being described, as in *kitchenette* (suffix "-ette") or *booklet* (suffix "-let").

The diminutive yet amazing basketball player proved the axiom "Good things do come in small packages."

discombobulate (DISS-kum-BAH-byoo-late), verb
To throw someone into a state of confusion; to utterly take aback. A great word to use, but don't confuse, or you will discombobulate or give someone the blues.

The attempt to see everything at Disneyland in one day can discombobulate even the calmest parents.

disconcerting (diss-kon-SER-ting), adjective
Causing unease, confusion, or dismay. Upsetting harmony or balance.

Many actions that are typical of teens are disconcerting to their parents and teachers.

disingenuous (dih-sen-JEN-yoo-wus), adjective
Less than honest, scheming, insincere, crafty, or sly. Withholding known information; intending to deceive. If dis or dat is less than genuine and honest, it is disingenuous.

Mary did not look Jim in the eye when she explained why she missed their date, so he suspected she was being disingenuous.

disparate (DISS-puh-rut), adjective

Things or people so dissimilar they cannot be compared. Two things fundamentally different. Do not confuse with *disparage*, which refers to disapproving; *desperate*, which means overwhelmed with anxiety to the point of losing hope; or *dissipate*, which is to cause something to disappear or evaporate.

Neil Simon's play The Odd Couple *was about two **disparate** men who learned their friendship could overcome all differences.*

disport (dih-SPORT), verb

To show off, draw attention to oneself, or behave in a playful way. If dis sport is a diversion, you're said to disport at a sporting event.

*Those two teens are acting like little kids as they **disport** at Disneyland.*

disseminate (dih-SEH-muh-nate), verb

To distribute or spread information or something else; to spread far and wide.

*Once information about colleges was received, the counselor had to decide how to **disseminate** the brochures and flyers.*

dissolution (dih-suh-LOO-shun), noun

The disintegration of a thing into fragments, parts, or smaller, more basic units. The destruction of an organization or institution; the breakup of a legal relationship, partnership, or marriage.

*The **dissolution** of the twenty-five-year marriage appeared sad to outsiders, but it made those involved feel happy and free.*

dissonance (DIH-suh-nunce), noun

Incompatibility among ideas, actions, or beliefs; disharmony between several sounds. The antonym of *consonance*, which means agreement, harmony, close similarity, or pleasing and simultaneous sounds. Dissonance is truly an annoyance, for it is disharmonious.

*Adolescence is often described as a period of **dissonance**, when young men and women face challenges, confusion, and conflict as they forge new beliefs that are often incompatible with past behaviors.*

dissuade (dih-SWADE), verb

To persuade someone against a course of action; to convince an audience not to think, feel, or believe a certain thing. To convince another to take alternate action.

*Tim's classmates **dissuaded** him from cutting class and risking a detention.*

DNA (dee enn AY), noun

The acronym for "deoxyribonucleic acid," the molecule that carries genetic information in all life forms. The workings of DNA are central concerns of biology and genetics.

DNA is commonly referred to as the "blueprint for life," for it carries the genetic codes associated with the post-fertilization development of an organism.

docile (DAW-sul), adjective

Quiet, easy to control or teach; unlikely to cause trouble. A crocodile is rarely docile.

*It is unusual to find a truly **docile** wolf, for these animals are wild by nature.*

dogmatic (dog-MA-tik), adjective

Strong expression or adherence to beliefs or opinions. Related to or expressing religious, political, philosophical, or moral dogma.

*Students believe some teachers are **dogmatic**, not willing to change their views or consider ideas counter to their own.*

domicile (DAH-muh-cile), noun

An occupied house, apartment, or residence; a legal, permanent home. Don't confuse it with docile, for a home is not easy to teach or control.

*Homeless individuals, by definition, have no **domicile**, so it is difficult if not impossible for them to get certain financial benefits.*

dossier (DOSS-yay), noun

A collection of documents related to a particular person or topic.

*The personnel office keeps a **dossier** on all employees.*

dot-com (doht-CAHM), noun
A company created to provide service or information over the World Wide Web. Also refers to Web sites on the Internet with the suffix ".com," compared to ".edu," ".org," or other suffixes.
*Initial public offerings, or the first public trading of stock in **dot-com** companies, created many instant millionaires.*

droll (DROLE), adjective
Amusing in a wry, odd, or funny way. Trolls might be droll, if they are funny and amusing.
*Norma's peers considered her **droll**, for she was always able to make them laugh with her offbeat comments.*

dyslexia (dis-LEK-see-uh), noun
A learning disorder marked by difficulty in spelling or reading.
*Her learning disabilities, including **dyslexia**, frequently caused her to transpose letters in words.*

ebullient (eh-BOOL-yunt), adjective
Full of cheer, enthusiasm, or optimism, as expressed in speech, writing, or behavior.
***Ebullient** game-show hosts are talented in very special ways.*

eccentricity (ek-sen-TRIH-suh-tee), noun
Unconventional, unpredictable, or erratic behavior or quality. The behavior of a person who is prone to odd behavior. A very fancy way of saying *strange,* and a word that often describes characters in novels. Remember Jay Gatsby?
*William was thought to be odd in general, but one of his **eccentricities**, his making of unusual noises, could have been a symptom of Tourette's syndrome.*

eclectic (eh-KLEK-tic), adjective
Made up of parts from various sources or origins; diverse items, styles, or things. Eclectic simply means *varied,* but using it in papers enhances your chances of earning better grades.
***Eclectic** musical tastes are unusual in teenagers, as they most often focus on the most popular groups or styles.*

edification (eh-dih-fuh-KAY-shun), noun
Instruction or enlightenment, often involving moral or spiritual teachings. Not a word to be confused with *edifice*, an impressive building or large complex structure, but similar to its soundalike, *education*.

*The evangelical preacher's **edification** of church members and others in the community was known to all.*

educe (ih-DOOCE), verb
To elicit, derive, or draw something out, often as in a logical conclusion. To reason or conclude from given facts. Related to *deduce*, which implies reaching a conclusion without all information, but not to *reduce*, which means to lessen.

*Myron's attempts to **educe** his sister's whereabouts were futile.*

effrontery (ih-FRON-tuh-ree), noun
An attitude or action notable for being bold, impudent, shameless, or arrogant. Effrontery in front of others is insulting.

*Sean had the **effrontery** to ask his parents for a new car immediately after he had an accident that was a result of drinking and driving.*

egalitarian (ih-ga-luh-TARE-ee-un), adjective
Related to or arising from a belief that all people are equal and should enjoy equal rights. Fair toward all parties. Not related to eagles, unless you believe that metaphorically all persons should be as free as these amazing birds.

*It is unusual to see **egalitarian** behavior among high school students, who often act as if rights are related to grade, age, and how cool someone seems.*

egocentric (EE-go-SEN-trik), adjective
Selfish; interested only in oneself, and not in the needs or feelings of others. Narrow-mindedly focused on self rather than other people. Sounds like *eccentric*, and while egocentrics can be odd or unusual, the two words are not synonyms—you shouldn't confuse them.

*Not surprisingly, the **egocentric** author's greatest achievement was an autobiography.*

egregious (ih-GREE-juss), adjective
Incorrect to an extraordinary level. Bad in a flagrant, blatant, or ridiculous way.

An egregious error is one so obvious it should not have been made, nor should it be easily forgiven.

elicit (ih-LIH-sit), verb
To cause, produce, or bring out a reaction. To evoke, stimulate, or generate a response. Too often confused with *illicit,* which means improper or illegal. While something illicit can elicit a reaction from the police, these two words are not synonyms.

*The calling of each graduate's name **elicited** cheers and applause from family and friends.*

elocution (eh-luh-KYOO-shun), noun
A manner or style of speaking, especially public speaking; the art of speaking well in public. *Elocution* refers to the way language is spoken; *eloquence* refers to the way ideas are expressed.

*The candidate's **elocution** was so poor that it diminished her ability to convey a coherent message.*

eloquence (EH-luh-kwents), noun
The ability to speak forcefully, expressively, and persuasively. Convincing and pleasant language.

*The professor's **eloquence** made her very popular among students and, ultimately, led to her being granted tenure.*

elucidate (ih-LOO-si-date), verb
To explain, clarify, or provide key information. To throw light on and clarify a subject. Related to the adjective *lucid,* meaning emitting light, rational, or clear and easily understood. Ed would elucidate his feelings, transforming Stephanie into a lucid date.

*Only Jordan could **elucidate** upon his motivations and why he behaved in certain ways.*

elusive (ee-LOO-siv), adjective
Difficult to find, catch, understand, perceive, comprehend, or describe. Not easily recalled or understood. Though it sounds like *elucidate*, this word has an opposite meaning.

Elusive goals are often the sweetest to gain because you have to work so hard to obtain them.

emanate (EH-muh-nate), verb
To come from or come out of someone, something, or somewhere. To flow from a specific source.

The glow and heat that emanated from the fireplace made everyone feel warm and safe.

emancipate (ih-MAN-si-pate), verb
To free or liberate from slavery, restraint, oppression, or bondage.

Many young people feel that an eighteenth birthday has the power to emancipate them from their parents' rules.

embellish (ihm-BEH-lish), verb
To increase the beauty of something by adding ornaments. To improve in appearance by adornment. To exaggerate the facts of a matter to make its description more interesting.

Jim embellished his tale of almost catching an elusive catfish until it began to resemble the story of Ahab's quest for the great white whale.

empathize (EM-puh-thize), verb
To identify with and understand another's feelings, emotions, and challenges. Not to be confused or misused with *emphasize*, which means to stress or give importance to something.

The counselor tried to empathize with students in order to earn their trust.

emulate (EM-yoo-late), verb
To attempt to match or surpass someone or something by imitation. To act using another as a model. Emus emulate ostriches; one flightless bird mimicking another.

Young children definitely emulate older brothers or sisters, so siblings must pay attention to who is watching them.

endemic (en-DEH-mik), adjective
Indigenous to a certain place, region, or group, as in characteristics, species, or disease. Something that describes and is confined to a particular area. In contrast, *pandemic* means existing in a wide area, such as in many countries.

*Pines of that type were **endemic** to only a specific region, one that was clearly identifiable by what was called the treeline.*

enervate (EH-nur-vate), verb
To weaken someone's physical, mental, or moral vitality. To deprive or diminish vitality, strength, or endurance. The antonym of *energize,* it is still sometimes misused to mean pepping somebody up when in fact it means bringing that person down.

*Activity-packed family vacations that are intended to provide rest and recuperation often **enervate** all involved.*

enigma (ih-NIG-ma), noun
Someone or something that is not easily explained; that which is puzzling, perplexing, inexplicable, or ambiguous. Enigmas, dilemmas, mysteries, and conundrums all involve situations that are difficult to explain or solve.

*The Mona Lisa's smile is probably the most popular **enigma** in the world of art.*

en masse (on MASS), adverb
As a body or group; together. A French term that translates loosely as "in the form of a crowd." Definitely try this one in your next conversation or paper, and then see the reactions. They will be positive en masse.

*Teenage girls seem to move **en masse**, almost always in a group.*

enmesh (en-MESH), verb
To involve, entangle, or implicate someone in a way that makes it hard for them to extricate themselves. Literally, it means to catch with a mesh net. Enmeshed in mesh nets, it was hard for fish to get loose.

*When Julie got home, she was immediately **enmeshed** in the raging argument between her brother and sister.*

enmity (EN-mi-tee), noun

Extreme ill will, hatred, and mutual antagonism between enemies. Not to be confused with *enigma*, which means a mystery, puzzle, or confusing person or thing. Sadly, it is a powerful and applicable word, today and every day.

*The **enmity** between terrorists and those they consider enemies grows day by day.*

enshrine (en-SHRINE), verb

To protect and preserve from change; to cherish as though sacred.

*The most significant honor an athlete can receive is to be **enshrined** in a sport's hall of fame.*

enthralling (ihn-THRALL-ing), adjective

Delightful, fascinating, or engaging someone's attention; beautiful, captivating, mesmerizing, or spellbinding.

*For most teenage boys, the beauty of swimsuit models is **enthralling**, to say the least.*

enunciate (ee-NUN-see-ate), verb

To pronounce distinctly; articulate. To give a speech that explains something clearly and lucidly. When you enunciate, you also elucidate and educate, so don't wait.

*The speech therapist worked with Sam on his inability to properly **enunciate** words that began with the letter T.*

Where'd That Word Come From?

Epicure—The ancient Greek philosopher Epicurus argued that true pleasure means peace of mind and freedom from want and pain, to be achieved through noble thoughts, self-control, and moderation. Students distorted his teachings completely, using them as an excuse for selfish indulgence, so that an epicure became one devoted to gluttony and debauchery. Centuries later, the word took on its current meaning of gourmet or connoisseur, one with refined tastes and knowledge of food and drink.

epicure (EH-pih-kyoor), noun

Someone with a refined taste for food and drink; a connoisseur. An epicure often needs an epic cure for heartburn and hangovers, even after eating good food and drinking fine wines.

*To an **epicure**, a fast food restaurant is an affront and not worthy of discussion.*

epiphany (ih-PIH-fuh-nee), noun

A sudden intuitive leap of understanding, often with credit given to divine inspiration. A sudden manifestation of the essence or meaning of something; a revelation. When capitalized, refers to the Christian festival celebrating the manifestation of Christ to the Gentiles.

*Seemingly miraculous circumstances, such as an unexplained recuperation from serious illness, often lead a person to an **epiphany** regarding the blessings of life.*

equanimity (ee-kwa-NIH-muh-tee), noun

Even temper and calm, usually displayed under stress; composure in a difficult situation. Not to be confused with *equality,* to value all in a group equally, or *anonymity,* the state of being unknown or not identifiable.

***Equanimity** is a quality to be revered and one that can be taught, practiced, and perfected.*

equinox (EE-kwih-noks), noun

Either of the two days in a year when the sun crosses the celestial equator and day and night are approximately equal.

*The vernal **equinox** occurs in the spring, and the autumnal **equinox** occurs in the fall.*

eradicate (ih-RA-dih-cate), verb

To destroy, get rid of, or do away with utterly. To wipe a thing out, leaving no sign, so it cannot recur or return.

*It is the greatest hope of many medical researchers to **eradicate** cancer within the next twenty years.*

ersatz (EHR-sats), adjective
Being an imitation or substitute for something of better quality. Character-istic of an unconvincing substitute that is not the real deal. If you err and sit on the ersatz chair, you might fall and hurt your derriere.

*Margarine is really just **ersatz** butter, so it doesn't taste as good.*

erudite (AIR-yoo-dite), adjective
Having or showing extensive knowledge gained from studying and reading; learned and scholarly. A person with either subject-specific knowledge or a broad and well-rounded education. Airheads are the opposite of erudite.

*Once you complete college, one should at least be able to describe you as **erudite**.*

esoteric (eh-suh-TARE-ik), adjective
Intended to be understood by a select and initiated few. Secret or highly con-fidential; accessible to insiders only. Using the word *esoteric* is quite esoteric. Get it? If so, you're among the select few who do!

***Esoteric** historians are not overly popular among college freshmen, but senior history majors tend to like them.*

espouse (ihs-POWZ), verb
To adopt, support, or advocate a particular belief or cause. Also, to take in marriage.

*Presidential candidates tend to **espouse** centrist causes as the election draws nearer.*

estrange (iss-TRANGE), verb
To cause someone to stop feeling friendly, affectionate, or sympathetic; to alienate or remove from a relationship.

*Today it is not unusual for family members to be **estranged**, either not living with or not caring about each other.*

etymology (eh-tih-MAH-luh-gee), noun
The study of word origins and how words have evolved into their current forms or meanings. The lineage of a word; description of origin and how the word came into its current use.

*Those who have studied Greek or Latin can make educated and often correct guesses regarding a word's **etymology**.*

euphemism (YOO-fuh-mih-zum), noun
A word or phrase used in place of another because it is less direct, unpleasant, offensive, or blunt. A nice way of saying something harsh, offensive, or vulgar.

You say these are going to be times of challenge for this company; isn't that just a **euphemism** *for times of decreased profitability?*

evanescent (EH-vuh-NEH-sent), adjective
Disappearing after only a short time; likely to vanish, like vapor. The name of a popular musical group, this word also describes the fate of most such groups.

Some stellar phenomena appear to astronomers, even those using the most sophisticated equipment, as **evanescent** *events, visible for only fractions of seconds.*

evoke (ih-VOKE), verb
To bring to mind a memory or feeling from the past, one that carries a particular reaction or feeling.

For college freshmen, first visits back to high school **evoke** *many positive memories and sentimental feelings.*

exacerbate (ig-ZA-sur-bate), verb
To worsen or aggravate an already bad situation. To make something even more unpleasant or severe.

Lying almost always **exacerbates** *a bad situation; that's one reason that honesty is the best policy.*

exculpate (ECK-skul-pate), verb
To free from blame or accusation of guilt. To clear one's name.

DNA evidence has been used to **exculpate** *those accused and convicted of many serious crimes.*

exhort (ig-ZORT), verb
To urge someone strongly and earnestly to follow a course of action. To give urgent or earnest advice.

Some believe it is an axiom that a crowd of cheering fans can **exhort** *players to achieve their maximum capability.*

exigency (eck-ZIH-jen-see), noun

An urgent situation requiring immediate action or attention. An unexpected development that puts pressure on those involved. An exigency sounds like its near synonym, *emergency*. Don't confuse with the meaning of the adjective *exiguous*, which means scanty or meager.

When the woman on the plane complained of labor pains, the flight attendant fully understood the **exigency** *of the situation.*

exonerate (ig-ZAH-nuh-rate), verb

Officially declare someone not guilty of a crime or blameless for an act. To relieve someone from obligation or responsibility. Similar to *exculpate*, but used in an official context.

The jury **exonerated** *him of any guilt in the case, but many people believed he was still somehow responsible.*

expeditious (eck-spuh-DIH-shuss), adjective

Speedy, prompt, and efficient.

My **expeditious** *completion of all chores meant I could leave the house immediately after dinner.*

expletive (EK-splih-tive), noun

An exclamation, interjection, or profanity. In grammar, the part of speech that conveys or expresses emotion without having a strict literal meaning, as in *Oh!* or *Ah ha!*

One of the editor's jobs was to expurgate **expletives** *from the manuscript in order to make the final copy acceptable to all readers.*

expurgate (ECK-spur-GATE), verb

To cleanse something, like a book or music lyrics, of material that is vulgar, obscene, or otherwise objectionable. A very fancy way to say *censor*.

The Federal Communications Commission motivates broadcasters to **expurgate** *offensive material by levying fines on stations that receive complaints from listeners.*

extenuate (ick-STEN-yoo-ate), verb

To make a mistake, fault, or error seem less serious by providing mitigating excuses.

Dylan managed to **extenuate** *his tardiness and avoid a week's detention.*

extrapolate (ick-STRA-puh-late), verb
To use known facts as a starting point, and then draw conclusions about something unknown. To estimate by examining unknown values that fall outside a range of known variables.

*Crime scene investigators are known for their abilities to **extrapolate** information about a victim's last hours, based upon forensic evidence.*

facet (FA-sit), noun
A component, dimension, or aspect; one of several parts. One face of a cut stone or smooth, polished surface.

*In order to do well on the history exam, Jay had to study all **facets** of the Civil War and the antebellum period.*

facetious (fa-SEE-shuss), adjective
Intended to be humorous, but often silly or inappropriate. Playful and communicated in jest. That which is frivolous or wryly humorous is facetious.

*Parents are being **facetious** when they suggest that children whining about being bored should go play in traffic.*

facilitate (fa-SIH-luh-TAYT), verb
To help along in order to make something easy, or easier to do. To decrease resistance in order to ease the flow of information, or the progress of someone or something.

*Web-based reservation systems **facilitate** the making of personal travel and vacation plans, diminishing the need for travel agents.*

fait accompli (FATE uh-com-PLEE), noun
Something done, decided, already concluded, or seemingly unalterable. From the French for "accomplished fact," an act or event presented as beyond change or dispute. While *done deal* is nice, "fait accompli" will suffice if you wish to impress teachers and others.

*Applying to some colleges for early decision means that if admitted, it is a **fait accompli** that you will attend.*

F

fastidious (fa-STIH-dee-uss), adjective
Concerned over the perfection of even the smallest detail. Meticulous and exacting; compulsive in terms of cleanliness.

*Robbie's mom is known as a **fastidious** housekeeper, so we all took our shoes off at the door.*

fatuous (FA-choo-uss), adjective
Revealing a lack of intelligence, as well as a lack of awareness. Stupid, foolish, or idiotic; without personal responsibility. Many teens are fatuous when expressing what they think is humor.

*Comedians that are **fatuous**, rather than thoughtfully sarcastic or clever, are not funny or worthy of their audience's approval.*

faux pas (foe PAW), noun
An embarrassing social blunder; a behavioral error. French for "false step." Stepping on kitty's four paws is clearly a faux pas.

*To avoid committing a **faux pas**, Wendi read several etiquette books before embarking on her trip to Europe.*

feckless (FEK-less), adjective
Unable or unwilling to do anything useful. Lacking the thought or organization necessary to succeed. Ineffective or feeble. Without initiative or ability in a specific field.

*It is frustrating when the most vocal person in a group of volunteers also proves to be the most **feckless**.*

felicity (fih-LIH-suh-tee), noun
Happiness, contentment, and bliss. Something that inspires sublime contentment. An appropriate or pleasing manner. Use this word in lieu of *happiness,* and those around you will be felicitous.

*The baby's after-meal **felicity** was a relief to his tired mother.*

feral (FEER-uhl), adjective
Having the qualities of a wild beast; undomesticated. Feral ferrets are fearsome, so watch out.

*Legends of **feral** children, those reared by wolves or apes, are common in folklore and literature.*

fervor (FUR-vur), noun
The extreme intensity of an emotion or belief. An intense craze or state of emotion. An abnormally high temperature. Similar to but not to be confused with *fever.*

Overcome by the fervor of the game, not the heat, the players on the winning team took off their jerseys and threw them to the crowd.

fiasco (fee-ASS-koe), noun
A total, humiliating, or ludicrous failure.

It was harsh, but accurate, to call their first date a fiasco, for both Barbara and Charles agreed to never speak to each other again.

Where'd That Word Come From?

Fiasco—This word, meaning "a total, foolish failure," derives from the Italian word *fiasco,* for "bottle," but no one seems to know why. Used in England as a theatrical term in the late nineteenth century, the word may have something to do with a bottle breaking—either accidentally or as part of the plot—in some forgotten yet very bad play. It might also be that a brand of wine in some bottles was flat or sour—a complete failure or fiasco—or that imperfect bottles made by glassblowers were called *fiascos.*

---

filibuster (FIH-luh-BUS-ter), noun
The use of delaying tactics to prevent things from getting done in a legislative assembly. Obstructionist tactics, especially prolonged speeches, whose purpose is to delay legislative action.

James Stewart gained fame, as well as an Oscar nomination, for his filibuster in the movie Mr. Smith Goes to Washington.

flaunt (FLONT), verb
To display in an ostentatious way; to lack shame, modesty, or humility. To show off a characteristic or possession in an outrageous way. Not to be confused, as often happens, with *flout* (defined on the next page).

Rappers flaunt their income with what they call "bling," and what others call ostentatious jewelry.

F

fledgling (FLEJ-ling), noun
A young bird whose flight feathers have just grown in. A young or inexperienced person. The fledging of the fledgling's feathers forecast flight for that night.

The fledgling golfer became frustrated after most shots but quite excited when a ball landed close to the hole.

flippant (FLIH-punt), adjective
Showing a lack of appropriate seriousness. A disrespectful disregard for decorum, often expressed by tactless chatter and jabber. Being flip to his aunt was thought flippant by his uncle and earned Joe punishment.

His flippant actions and words earned a few laughs from his peers, but they also got him several days of detention and a bad reputation.

flout (FLOUT), verb
To show contempt by openly breaking a law, rule, or tradition. Fools flout the rules in front of police and end up in jail.

Leaving one's hat on during the playing of the national anthem flouts a tradition and it is considered highly disrespectful.

foible (FOI-bull), noun
An idiosyncrasy, small weakness, failing, fault, or character flaw that is comparatively insignificant.

A common foible is to surround yourself with those who flatter, rather than those who will be honest.

foist (FOYST), verb
To unload something undesirable, false, or inferior on the pretence that it is genuine, valuable, or desirable; to pawn off something undesirable.

This project was foisted off on us because everyone believed it was impossible and because we were considered the worst department in the organization.

foray (FORE-ay), noun
An initial attempt at a new activity or occupation. A short trip or visit to a place; a particular purpose. A sudden military attack or raid.

Elizabeth's foray into the world of publishing was not without some disheartening moments.

fortuitous (fore-TOO-uh-tuss), adjective
By chance, accidental; lucky or fortunate. Unplanned but yielding a pleasant outcome.

*After years of trial and error, Dr. Powers made a **fortuitous** discovery when he mistakenly combined two chemical compounds.*

fractious (FRAK-shuss), adjective
Irritable and quarrelsome. Likely to misbehave or complain; unruly. Likely to cause disturbance or trouble. Not related in meaning to *fraction*, a number that is not a whole number or a small portion of an entire thing.

*For some strange reason, the saying "Boys will be boys" is often used to describe **fractious** male teens who act out in public.*

fruition (froo-IH-shun), noun
The point at which something comes to maturity or reaches a desired outcome. The achievement of something desired or labored. Literally and figuratively, "to reap the fruit of one's labors."

*All those years of studying reached **fruition** when Ted was accepted to the college he had dreamed of.*

fulminate (FUL-mih-nate), verb
To criticize or denounce loudly, dramatically, or forcefully. In another sense, to detonate an explosion.

*By now, we had all grown tired of listening to our father **fulminating** against "those crooked politicians."*

funereal (fyoo-NIR-ee-uhl), adjective
Reminiscent of, related to, or suitable for a funeral. Solemn, mournful, dark, brooding, and dismal. Clearly a very dramatic adjective—just be careful to spell it correctly, or you may be mournful.

*After they lost the state championship, the football team's locker room could be accurately described as **funereal**.*

furtive (FUR-tiv), adjective
Surreptitious, sly, stealthy; meant to escape detection. Describes a person with something to hide. High school students are furtive in many circumstances because they often have something to hide. So you can use this fancy word on numerous occasions.

Prior to the surprise party, Stacy's friends appeared furtive as they made plans, purchased gifts, and transported supplies.

fussbudget (FUSS-buh-jet), noun
Someone who typically worries about trivial things. A word most famously applied to Charlie Brown's friend Lucy.

Most fussbudgets seem to have an unlimited supply of fuss and bother because they never run out of either.

fuzzy-headed (FUH-zee HED-ehd), adjective
Not thinking clearly, or not expressing ideas or thoughts clearly; inarticulate.

A fuzzy-headed morning often follows a fun night.

gallantry (GAL-luhn-tree), noun
Courtesy, thoughtfulness, and bravery; nobility or chivalry, especially in actions toward women. Grand, majestic, or showy dress, style, or action.

Some say that chivalry and gallantry are dead, but if you look hard you can see that they are still alive and well in many modern attitudes and actions.

galumph (ga-LUMF), verb
To walk or run in a clumsy and boisterous way. To move heavily, with thudding steps.

Today's athletes galumph in triumph after a touchdown, basket, or goal; they have no concern for the sportsmanship of the past.

galvanize (GAL-vuh-nize), verb
To stimulate someone or something into action, especially muscle fibers, by means of electric current. In a technical sense, to coat a metal with zinc to prevent corrosion.

The hardships of winter galvanize the isolated residents of Maine to help one another whenever needed.

gamesmanship (GAYMZ-muhn-ship), noun
Strategies used to gain an advantage in sports, life, business, or politics. Unconventional but not strictly illegal tactics employed to gain an advantage.

*Pre-game chatter with opposing team members is a sure sign of **gamesmanship**, and it can backfire at times.*

gamut (GA-mut), noun
The full range or extent. A critic once famously slammed an early performance of Katharine Hepburn's as running the "gamut of emotions from A to B." In music, refers to the entire series of standard musical notes.

*His house featured an entertainment center whose components ran the **gamut** of state-of-the-art equipment.*

garner (GAHR-ner), verb
To earn, acquire, collect, amass, gather, or accumulate something by effort. To gather something into storage.

*Jamie, always a good student, **garnered** many honors at commencement, including that of valedictorian.*

garnish (GAHR-nish), verb
To add something to food or drink to enhance flavor or appearance; to decorate something, usually food, with an ornament.

*Tony would **garnish** his wedding cakes with rose blossoms, enhancing their appearance as well as fragrance.*

garrulous (GAR-uh-lus), adjective
Excessively talkative; using many, many, many, too many words.

*Drunks are often described as **garrulous**.*

gastronomy (gas-TRAH-nah-mee), noun
The art or appreciation of preparing and eating good food. Those who practice gastronomy don't necessarily have gas, but their efforts do focus on things "gastro," relating to the stomach or belly.

*Those knowledgeable in **gastronomy** don't consider hot dogs bought and eaten at a sporting event to be epicurean delights, but true fans do.*

G

gauche (GOASH), adjective
Lacking grace or tact in a social situation. Describes a socially inappropriate remark or action.

Justin's constant belching at the table was clearly gauche, but he believed such behavior was normal for a teenager.

gaudy (GAHW-dee), adjective
Brightly colored, showy; decorated in a tasteless or vulgar way. Tacky or excessively ornamental.

Those who win the lottery or acquire other unexpected riches often quickly adorn themselves with gaudy jewelry.

genteel (jen-TEEL), adjective
Refined, good-mannered; typical of high social standing. Overdoing the refined behavior considered typical of the upper class. At the risk of provoking giggles, *please* do not confuse this well-mannered word with *genital*, which refers to external sexual organs.

Cynthia took care to make sure she ate properly and conversed politely at her first experience with her genteel future in-laws.

germane (jerr-MAYNE), adjective
Suitably related to something, especially the topic being discussed. Not to be confused with the noun *German*, which is someone raised and born in Germany, the official language of Germany, or something from Germany. The word "German" is only germane when you are speaking about Germany.

Let's see what Bill has to say, as his contributions are always germane.

gerrymander (JAIR-ee-MAN-der), verb
To divide an electoral district so as to give a political advantage to a particular party. To divide a geographic area into voting districts so as to give advantage to one party in elections.

The state legislature's attempt to gerrymander was deemed illegal and voided by the state supreme court.

gestation (jes-TAY-shun), noun
The carrying of offspring in the womb. The necessary period of time for the development of a fetus during pregnancy. Also, the development of a concept, idea, or plan. Not a "gas station," where you purchase gas.

*The **gestation** of one's candidacy for president begins well before and goes well beyond the primary elections.*

gesticulation (jes-TICK-yoo-lay-shun), noun
A movement of hands or arms that accompanies speech, usually for emphasis. An expression made with hands and arms, and not a vulgar one-finger gesture.

*Great orators are versed in **gesticulation** as well as verbal eloquence.*

gizmo (GIZZ-moe), noun
An overly complicated device, usually mechanical. A gadget is a gizmo, and a gizmo is a gadget. Yes, they are synonyms.

*Justin's father is always designing and building **gizmos** that cost more than things he could just get from the store.*

glasnost (GLAZ-noast), noun
A Soviet policy permitting greater openness, discussion, and disclosure of ideas and information. Used by Mikhail Gorbachev, former Soviet premier, to describe the less repressive policies of the Soviet Union in the 1980s.

*A period of **glasnost** preceded the downfall of the Soviet Union and foretold of an independent and democratic Russia.*

gloaming (GLOW-ming), noun
The time of fading light after sunset, just before dark.

*The **gloaming** is sometimes gloomy, but often serene.*

glossary (GLAU-suh-ree), noun
An alphabetical collection of specialist terms and meanings, often an appendix to a book—or, in the case of this publication, an entire book.

*A **glossary** is a special list for specialists, containing words and definitions.*

glutton (GLUH-tuhn), noun

Someone who eats and drinks to excess, or who overindulges in a particular behavior.

*For Terri to keep misbehaving like that, she must be a **glutton** for punishment.*

goad (GODE), verb

To provoke, invite, stimulate, urge, or prod, especially toward a specific action. Originally, the word meant a pointed stick used to prod animals.

*As a form of initiation, or hazing, members of the football team would **goad** freshmen into running naked across the field.*

goliath (guh-LIE-uth), noun

Something or someone large in size and stature; giant. When capitalized, refers to the biblical giant who was slain by David with a sling and stone.

*The **goliath** sundae, made with four flavors of ice cream and five toppings, was too large for one person to finish.*

gossipmonger (GOHS-sip-MOHN-guhr), noun

Someone who conducts a conversation about personal or intimate rumors or facts, especially those that are malicious to and about others.

*Stacie was a notorious **gossipmonger**, yet she still had the ears of many in the twelfth grade.*

gradation (gray-DAY-shun), noun

A series of gradual and progressive degrees, steps, or stages. A move that is made in measured, distinct stages. Gradation is gradual progress, and not to be confused with *graduation*, which is often the result of a four-year process.

*The **gradation** of colors in the sunset covered the whole range of the spectrum.*

graft (GRAFT), noun

The use of dishonest or illegal means to gain money or property, often by someone in a position of power or elected office. Personal profit made in an illicit way because of official standing.

*The game had been sold out for months, and the mayor's easy acquisition of choice tickets led to whisperings of **graft** in the administration.*

grandeur (GRAN-jur), noun
The quality of being great, grand, or very impressive; extravagance in scale or appearance.

*The **grandeur** of Buckingham Palace impresses all who have the honor to visit.*

grandiloquence (gran-DIH-luh-kwence), noun
A pompous or lofty manner of speech. Bombast; language that is full of long, pretentious words. Also an attitude of haughtiness.

*Politicians in love with their own **grandiloquence** may not always be good at solving problems and keeping campaign promises.*

grandiose (GRAN-dee-OCE), adjective
Pretentious, pompous, and imposing. Can be used to describe pretensions or ambitions that go beyond abilities or means.

*It is surprising when **grandiose** schemes become realities, but that is why so many reach for the stars.*

gratuitous (gra-TOO-ih-tuss), adjective
Unnecessary, out of place, excessive, and unjustifiable. Received or given without payment or charge.

***Gratuitous** violence and nudity has become prevalent in movies and video games.*

gravitas (GRAH-vih-tahs), noun
A serious and solemn attitude or way of behaving.

*A funeral is an appropriate place for **gravitas**.*

gregarious (gri-GARE-ee-uss), adjective
Very friendly, sociable, outgoing, or cordial; happy in the company of others.

***Gregarious** individuals are often suspected of having hidden agendas when they are really just being friendly.*

grisly (GRIHS-lee), adjective
Gruesomely unpleasant or creating a sense of horror. Not to be confused with *grizzly*, which is a type of bear.

*Seeing grizzlies eating the carcasses of their prey is a **grisly** sight.*

H

grovel (GRAH-vul), verb
To act in a servile way. To show exaggerated and false respect, intending to please or out of fear. To crawl or lie face down in humility or fear.

Prisoners were forced to grovel before their guards, fearing torture and abuse if they did not.

guffaw (guh-FAWE), noun
A loud and raucous laugh.

Robert's guffaw was embarrassing to his wife, so she grimaced whenever they went to a humorous play.

guile (GILE), noun
Cunning, deceitful, and treacherous quality or type of behavior. Skill and cleverness used to trick, deceive, or mislead people.

No matter how smart you think you are, you are no match for the guile of an experienced street con seeking to separate you from your money.

Where'd That Word Come From?

Haggard—This words originates with the 3,000-year-old sport of falconry. A haggard bird is one trapped as an adult and very difficult to train, unlike a bird captured as a nestling. The word came to mean a wild, intractable person, and it later took on the meaning of a terrified, anxious, or exhausted expression on a human face. This finally evolved to mean gaunt, drawn, wasted, or exhausted.

---

hackneyed (HAK-need), adjective
Made commonplace, less significant, and stale by overuse or common use. Strictly, refers either to a carriage for hire or to a horse suited only for routine riding or driving.

Soap operas are now hackneyed caricatures of dramas appearing on television daily.

haggard (HA-gurd), adjective
Showing signs of tiredness, anxiety, or hunger. Wild and unruly in appearance.
*After a twelve-hour shift at the hospital, anyone would look **haggard**.*

halcyon (HAL-see-on), adjective
Tranquil, prosperous, carefree; free from disturbance The word also refers to a bird related to the kingfisher, which in myth could calm ocean storms.
*The company's **halcyon** years were behind it; all was in chaos now.*

hale (HAYL), adjective
In robust good health. Used most often in the phrase "hale and hardy." A robust word to use in writing or speech.
*After recovering from a bout of flu, Mitch was finally feeling **hale** again.*

halitosis (HA-lih-toe-sis), noun
A formal and fancy way of referring to very bad breath. If you use this word about your friend it might not embarrass him as much; on the other hand, if he had used a mint, you wouldn't have to use this word at all.
*Knowing about Skip's **halitosis**, I decided to wait for the next elevator after I saw him get on one.*

hallmark (HAWL-mahrk), noun
A mark showing something is of high quality, or one identifying purity of certain metals or the maker of specific crafted items. A feature of something that distinguishes it from similar items. No, it's not just a type of greeting card. The hallmark of Mark's hall was an amazing mural.
*Each college has a building that serves as a **hallmark** of that institution.*

Where'd That Word Come From?

Hallmark—These "marks of excellence on products," originated as the official stamp of the Goldsmiths' Company of London. In 1300, Edward I ordered that all gold and silver be struck with such a mark to indicate its purity. They were called *hallmarks* because the stamping was done at Goldsmiths' Hall in London.

hallow (HA-low), verb

To make someone or something holy. To have great respect or reverence, the highest possible honor for a person or thing.

*Many football fans **hallow** the frozen tundra of Lambeau Field where the Green Bay Packers play.*

halo effect (HAY-low ih-FEKT), noun

The tendency to judge someone as being totally good because one particular aspect of his or her character is good, or because those around him or her are also good.

*The **halo effect** helps us assume that young men and women who sing in church choirs and participate in church youth groups are free of behavioral problems, but it's not always true.*

hamlet (HAM-luht), noun

A small village or group of houses, homesteads, or households. Not just the name of Shakespeare's melancholy Dane. If you describe certain residences as a hamlet, it will be quite quaint and impress your readers or listeners.

*During their summer trip to North Carolina, the Harrisons visited many **hamlets** and stayed at some phenomenal bed-and-breakfast inns.*

haphazard (hap-HA-zurd), adjective

Happening or done in a way not planned; irregular; governed by chance. Something not guided by a regular or predetermined method. Haphazard golfers often happen to be in a hazard.

*After several rounds using a **haphazard** approach to the game, Mark decided that golf lessons were definitely in order.*

hapless (HA-pluss), adjective

Unlucky, unfortunate, or inauspicious. Haphazard hunters may appear hapless, but a little planning may give them better luck.

*High school freshmen seem so **hapless** during the first few weeks of school, but they later appear more confident.*

harangue (huh-RANG), verb
To rant. To criticize or question in a very loud, forceful or angry way. To scold sternly, often openly in public. It's embarrassing when harangued about poorly baked meringue.

*Peter's parents would regularly **harangue** him regarding inappropriate dress and behavior, but it never seemed to help.*

harbinger (HAR-bin-jur), noun
Someone or something that brings about a major change. One that foreshadows or anticipates something still to come.

*Employment figures are accepted as **harbingers** of economic trends and, during election years, of political success or failure.*

haughty (HAW-tee), adjective
Superior, condescending, or arrogant. Rather than using the "B" word, it's more polite to describe someone as haughty.

*The **haughty** behavior of those who were members of the country club was not appreciated by their friends.*

haute cuisine (OAT kwi-ZEEN), noun
Traditional, classic, high-quality French cooking or general gourmet preparation of food. Can refer to the preparation of meals like artwork.

*Gourmets, though not necessarily gourmands, prefer **haute cuisine**, because they believe more in quality rather than quantity.*

HAZMAT (HAZ-maht), abbreviation
Stands for "hazardous material." The label given a team of professionals who deal with hazardous material.

*More than ever, **HAZMAT** training and team members are critical.*

hearsay (HEER-say), adjective
Describing information that is heard from other people, and not from the person or persons who made the original statement. Information gained from another party, not as a result of observing the original action.

***Hearsay** evidence is not admissible in a court of law.*

hegemony (hih-JEH-muh-nee), noun

Control or dominating influence by one person or group over others; dominance. Most often the dominance of one political group over society, or one nation over another. Predominant influence, especially in reference to the affairs of nations. To say one nation practices hegemony over another is to suggest that it exercises undue influence over conduct, mores, or administration within that nation.

*England has throughout history been accused of trying to achieve **hegemony**, particularly with regard to past members of the British Empire.*

heinous (HAY-nuss), adjective

Shockingly wicked, evil, or reprehensible. Far exceeding the norms of morality.

*Because of the **heinous** nature of terrorist attacks, the world has united against those committing these evil acts.*

heirloom (ARE-lume), noun

Something valuable handed down from one generation to the next. An item that is a part of an estate, with a legal heir to inherit it. An ancient hair loom, used to make hair rugs, could be a valued heirloom.

*The cameo brooch that Mrs. Powell wore was an **heirloom** passed on by her grandmother to her mother and from her mother to her.*

heraldry (HEHR-uhl-dree), noun

The practice of creating coats of arms and determining those who are entitled to bear them. Coats of arms and symbols associated with specific birth rights. Pomp and ceremony.

*The study of medieval **heraldry** can be fascinating.*

herbivorous (EHR-bihv-rus), adjective

Eating only grass and plants, not meat. An antonym of *carnivorous*.

*Even **herbivorous** dinosaurs would have been intimidating by virtue of their size, though not necessarily their eating habits.*

herculean (hur-kyuh-LEE-un), adjective
Strong and powerful; relating to or resembling Hercules. Daunting, formidable, extremely difficult, requiring a great deal of strength, stamina, effort, or resources.

*The **herculean** efforts of the 1969 Mets to win the World Series will go down in baseball history.*

herstory (HER-steh-ree), noun
History presented from a feminist perspective or with an emphasis on the point of view of women. The study or recording of life experiences, achievements, or ambitions of a particular woman or group of women. A new word that originated in the feminist lexicon, yet is now commonly used.

*The **herstory** of the women's suffrage movement is in many ways the story of Susan B. Anthony's life.*

heterogeneous (heh-teh-ruh-JEE-nee-us), adjective
Consisting of unrelated parts or elements. Different and not related.

*While admissions offices do admit many students with similar profiles, a college is still a **heterogeneous** and diverse community.*

heyday (HAY-day), noun
The time of someone's or something's greatest popularity, success, or power.

*While it was thought that the 1960s were the **heyday** of the bell-bottom, this fashion trend seems to be making a revival today.*

hiatus (hie-AY-tuss), noun
A break in something where there should be continuity; an interruption or gap.

*After his refusal to submit to the draft and his long **hiatus** from boxing, Muhammad Ali returned to the ring and won back the heavyweight title.*

hierarchy (HIE-eh-rahr-kee), noun
An organization or group with members arranged by ranks, in order of seniority or power. Categorization by order of importance or status. A normal chain of command. Originally referred to the division of angels into ranks.

*The military **hierarchy** is clear and obvious by title and uniform.*

hindsight (HYND-syte), noun
The realization or analysis of an event after it has happened. Perception of the past, in retrospect.

Hindsight is twenty-twenty, and lessons learned by analyzing history should prove valuable when planning for the future.

histrionic (hiss-tree-ON-ick), noun
Overdramatic in reaction or behavior; theatrical. Related to acting or actors.

The histrionics associated with two adolescents breaking up is hard for adults to deal with.

HIV (AYCH eye vee), acronym
Acronym for "human immunodeficiency virus." Refers to a retrovirus that destroys the immune system and causes AIDS (acquired immune deficiency syndrome).

Although we are working hard to discover a cure for HIV, we must continue to be careful about sexually transmitted diseases.

hoax (HOACKS), verb
To trick someone into believing something is real when it is not.

They hoaxed us by burying false fossils in the old excavation site.

holistic (ho-LISS-tik), adjective
Involving all of something; specifically, all of someone's physical, mental, and social conditions, not just the physical when treating an illness.

Holistic medicine, addressing all contributing factors of illness, is increasingly popular.

homage (AH-mij), noun
Show of reverence, honor, and respect; a formal public acknowledgment, reverence, allegiance, or honor.

By visiting the lacrosse hall of fame, the team paid homage to the sport they played.

hominid (HAH-muh-nid), noun
A primate belonging to a particular biological family, all extinct except for modern human beings. Humans and their ancestors.

*The more archeologists and anthropologists study, the more they agree that Africa was the birthplace of **hominids**.*

homonym (HAH-muh-nim), noun
A word that sounds and is spelled the same as another word but with a different meaning.

*"Tee fore too" and "tea for two" are phrases full of **homonyms**.*

hubris (HYOO-briss), noun
Excessive pride or arrogance. The excessive pride and ambition that often leads to the downfall of a hero in a classical tragedy. Hubris can refer to the "fatal flaw" of ancient Greek drama, or, generally, to any disproportionate pride or self-love.

*It was clear that the immaturity and **hubris** displayed by many dot-com millionaires led to the downfall of their companies and the financial woes of many shareholders.*

hyperbole (hie-PUR-buh-lee), noun
Deliberate and obvious exaggeration used for effect; an extravagant overstatement.

*The **hyperbole** associated with being worth one's weight in gold is one that some would like to test in reality.*

hypothermia (hie-po-THER-mee-uh), noun
Dangerously low body temperature caused by prolonged exposure to cold; extreme loss of body heat. From the Greek for "below heat."

*Most of the fatalities associated with the sinking of the Titanic were as a result of **hypothermia**.*

Iberian (EYE-beer-ee-uhn) noun
Someone who lives or was born or raised in Spain or Portugal, or one who lived on the Iberian Peninsula.

*While **Iberians** share a common geography, those from Spain and Portugal want to be perceived as a unique people.*

ichthus (ICK-thaas), noun
A simple symbol of Christianity that resembles a fish, consisting of two curves that bisect each other.

*People sometimes put **ichthus** bumper stickers on their cars, often to let others know they are born-again Christians.*

iconoclast (eye-kah-nuh-KLAST), noun
Someone who challenges or overturns traditional customs, beliefs, and values.

Iconoclasts are always controversial, and often they are perceived as dangerous.

Where'd That Word Come From?

Iconoclast—This word for a debunker, one who attacks cherished beliefs, dates from the time of Byzantine emperor Leo III, who in 726 began a program of destroying icons, or images, in churches because he believed his people actually worshipped the icons, not the religious figures they represented. The monks fanatically opposed Leo and called him, among other things, an *iconoclast*, "image breaker."

ideology (EYE-dee-ah-luh-gee), noun
A closely organized system of beliefs, values, and ideas, especially one that forms the basis of a social, economic, or political philosophy. A system of thought that shapes the way an individual group thinks, acts, and views the world. Not to be confused with *idolatry*, the worship of idols or false gods, or the extreme admiration or fanatical devotion to someone or something.

*For some extreme fans, Star Trek is the foundation of an **ideology** and not just a science fiction television show.*

idiom (IH-dee-uhm), noun
A phrase whose usage is peculiar to a particular language, in terms of grammar or in meaning. An expression whose meaning cannot be figured out from the grammatical combination of individual words, such as "He puts me in stitches." The way of using a language that comes naturally to native speakers and involves knowledge of grammar and usage.

*For the recent immigrant from Brazil, **idioms** such as "beating a dead horse" were quite difficult to understand and sometimes rather disturbing.*

idyllic (EYE-dih-lick), adjective
Serenely beautiful, untroubled, and happy. Like an idyll, which is a scene, event, or experience characterized by tranquility and simple beauty.

*As they arrived at the bed and breakfast at sunset, it seemed an **idyllic** place to stay for their honeymoon.*

ignominious (ig-nuh-MIH-nee-uss), adjective
Characterized by a total loss of dignity and pride; shamefully weak, ineffective, or disgraceful. Used to describe public humiliation or failure.

*Richard Nixon's **ignominious** resignation of the presidency will forever remind those in high office to be honest and not cover up errors in judgment.*

ignoramus (ig-nuh-RAY-muss), noun
An idiot, dolt, or someone who is ignorant.

*Someone who ignores his studying may not be smart, but he should not be called an **ignoramus**.*

illicit (ih-LIH-sit), adjective
Not allowed by law; wrong, unacceptable by prevailing standards; illegal or morally unjustifiable.

*Gains acquired by **illicit** activities often yield more guilt than wealth.*

imbibe (im-BIBE), verb
To drink something, especially alcohol or alcoholic beverages. To take in or absorb something into the mind, like an idea. It's hard to thrive when you regularly imbibe.

*Although it sounds better to say "**imbibe**" and "inebriated," you might just as well say "booze it up" and "drunk."*

imbroglio (im-BROAL-yo), noun

A confusing, messy, or complicated situation, especially one that involves disagreement or intrigue. An entanglement or complicated misunderstanding. Describes a delicate situation from which it is difficult to extricate oneself.

*Soap opera characters become entangled in one **imbroglio** after another, never learning from their mistakes.*

imbue (im-BYOO), verb

To saturate something with a substance, particularly a liquid or dye. To make something or someone rich with a particular quality, or to transmit an idea, feeling, or emotion.

*Good teachers seek to **imbue** students with the love of learning in addition to facts and subject knowledge.*

immigrant (ih-MIH-grunt), noun

Someone who comes to a country to settle there. Sounds like its antonym, *emigrant,* which is someone who leaves a place, especially his or her native land, to live in another country.

*Almost every American **immigrant** dreams of success, wealth, and happiness.*

imminent (ih-MUH-nent), adjective

About to happen, or threatening to happen. Not to be confused with its homonym, *immanent,* which means existing within or inherent in something, extending to all parts of the created world.

*Everyone knew that the victory was **imminent,** so they left the game early.*

immutable (IH-myoo-tuh-bull), adjective

Not changing, or not able to be changed.

*Some believe that criminals are truly **immutable** and cannot change their ways.*

impalpable (im-PAL-puh-bull), adjective

Not capable of being perceived with the sense of touch, or not capable of being perceived by the senses. Difficult to understand or grasp; difficult to perceive or interpret.

*The **impalpable** dark left him with only the vague impression that someone else had just left the room.*

impart (im-PART), verb
To give or bestow a particular quality upon something. To communicate information or knowledge.
*Professor Green daily sought to **impart** wisdom to his students.*

impasse (IM-pass), noun
A point or situation with no solution, or when no further progress can be made or agreement reached. A situation that seems to offer no solution or escape. A road or passage that has no way out: literally, a dead-end street or passage.
*The research team's efforts had come to an **impasse**, so they brought in new members to inspire innovative approaches.*

impeach (im-PEACH), verb
To charge a government official with serious misconduct while in office. To remove an official, including a president, from public office for having committed high crimes and misdemeanors. To make an accusation against, challenge the validity of, or discredit someone or some document.
*It is the responsibility of a good attorney to **impeach** the credibility of witnesses, although it often appears to be an aggressive and mean-spirited strategy.*

impeccable (im-PECK-uh-bull), adjective
Perfect, flawless; beyond criticism or sin. From the Latin for "without sin."
*While we may expect all priests to be morally **impeccable**, recent events prove that even they are human.*

imperative (im-PAIR-uh-tiv), adjective
Absolutely necessary, unavoidable, obligatory, or mandatory. Forceful and demanding obedience and respect.
*As the fire swept closer, it became **imperative** to evacuate.*

impertinence (im-PURR-tih-nent), noun
Boldness or rudeness; brash behavior showing a shocking lack of respect for a superior. Disrespectful action or comment. Inappropriate to a particular matter or issue.
*Too often confused with courage, **impertinence** is unacceptable in most circumstances.*

impervious (im-PUHR-vee-us), adjective
Remaining unmoved and unaffected by other's opinions or actions. Impossible to alter or affect; incapable of being diverted from a given course.

*Everyone knows Superman was **impervious** to pain, except that caused by Kryptonite.*

impetuous (im-PEH-choo-wus), adjective
Tending to act on the spur of the moment, without consideration of consequences. Impulsive; passionate. Characterized by great force and energy.

*Some believe the phrase "**impetuous** youth" is redundant, for acting without thinking is one way to define adolescence.*

impetus (IM-puh-tus), noun
The energy or motivation behind an accomplishment or undertaking. The force that causes the motion of an object to overcome resistance and maintain velocity.

*The **impetus** for Jorge's business successes seemed to be a quest for his father's approval.*

impinge (im-PINJ), verb
To strike or run into something, with force. To have an effect on something. Also, to encroach upon the limits of something, especially a right or law; to cause some kind of restriction.

*Censorship most definitely **impinges** on the right of free speech, which is why we hold the first amendment sacred.*

implicate (IM-pluh-kayt), verb
To show that someone or something played a part in or is connected to an activity, such as a crime. To imply or involve something as a consequence.

*Being at the scene of the vandalism wouldn't necessarily **implicate** anyone, but it would cast suspicion and motivate investigators to look further.*

implicit (im-PLIH-sit), adjective
Implied or understood, though not expressed directly. An understanding that parties abide by but do not set out in specific language.

*They had an **implicit** agreement not to bring up the subject of their huge fight of the year before.*

implore (im-PLORE), verb
To beg or pray for something fervently. To plead urgently.

*No matter how Bob **implored** her, the teacher would not allow him to make up the exam.*

imprudent (im-PROO-dent), adjective
Showing no care, forethought, or judgment. Lacking discretion. As a teenager, even dear Prudence was imprudent, always acting without thinking. (Not to be confused with *impudent,* which means lacking modesty, being contemptuous, or cocky.)

*Buying cigarettes and alcohol for her teenage friends was certainly **imprudent**, as well as illegal and improper.*

impugn (im-PYOON), verb
To suggest that someone or something cannot be trusted. To challenge someone's honesty or motives. Not to be confused with the next entry, *impunity*, which sounds alike but basically means "unable to be impugned."

*The defense attorney sought to **impugn** the prosecutor's witness.*

impunity (im-PYOO-nuh-tee), noun
Exemption from punishment, harm, penalty, or recrimination.

*It is feared that possessing wealth is the same as possessing **impunity**.*

in vitro (inn VEE-troe), adjective
An artificial environment, such as a test tube, rather than inside a living organism. Describes an egg that is fertilized outside of the mother and then implanted in the womb.

*In **vitro** fertilization is a miraculous procedure for those who thought they would never be able to conceive a child.*

inane (in-ANE), adjective
Having little sense or importance; empty, vacuous, unsubstantial, pointless, or lacking in meaning.

***Inane** comments are best ignored, even if they are made by someone who should know better.*

inarguable (in-ARG-yoo-uh-bull), adjective
Impossible to deny or take an opposing view from. The position of most parents, when a teenager comes home hours after curfew.

Alex's assertions regarding who manufactured a particular car model were inarguable.

inauspicious (ih-nah-SPIH-shuss), adjective
Suggesting that the future is not very promising or that success is unlikely. Marked by a sign of some kind that things might not work out as well as planned.

*The **inauspicious** beginning of their trip was marked by a speeding ticket and a flat tire, making them fear what would next go wrong.*

Where'd That Word Come From?
Inauspicious—Like many words used today, this word, meaning "unlikely to lead to success," made its debut in the works of Shakespeare. In *Romeo and Juliet*, Romeo cries: "Here, here, will I remain. And shake the yoke of inauspicious stars. From this world-wearied flesh." Shakespeare probably invented *inauspicious*, as he did *auspicious* (in *The Tempest*), meaning favorable, marked by lucky signs or good omens, conducive to success. Its roots are in the Latin *auspex*, a corruption of *avispex*, for the Roman birdwatcher who deduced omens from the flight of birds.

incendiary (in-SEN-dee-air-ee), adjective
Describes the deliberate burning of property. Designed to excite or inflame, as in causing civil unrest. Able to catch fire spontaneously or easily.

*His **incendiary** remarks were certainly not necessary, as the crowd was already emotionally charged.*

incessant (in-SEH-sunt), adjective
Continuing unstopped for a long time. From the Latin roots for "without end."

*The children's **incessant** singing on the bus gave the teacher and chaperone headaches.*

incipient (in-SEH-pee-unt), adjective
Beginning to appear or develop; at an early stage. Sounds like and shares a root with *inception*, the beginning of something.
Incipient bad behavior of puppies must be addressed quickly, as it quickly becomes difficult to change their habits.

incisive (in-SYE-siv), adjective
Quick to understand, analyze, or act. Sharp in analysis, observation, or action; from the Latin for "cutting."
Matt's incisive essay earned him an A, and it assured him a great grade point average for the semester.

incognito (in-cog-NEE-to), adjective
With one's identity disguised or hidden, as when using a false name. Describes the action of taking an assumed name or intentionally changing appearance and hiding from public recognition by making one's real identity unknown.
Rock stars, actors, and other famous people wear sunglasses and hats, seeking to be incognito at restaurants; these disguises rarely work, though, and they are often recognized.

incongruous (in-KAHN-groo-wus), adjective
Unsuitable, strange, not matching. Out of place in a particular context or setting; discordant. If you attended a formal wearing jeans with holes, you could say you felt incongruous, or you are a teen who shopped at Abercrombie.
The mourner's smiles and giggles were completely incongruous at the funeral.

incontrovertible (in-KAHN-truh-VER-tuh-bull), adjective
Certain, undeniable, and not open to question or controversy. Impossible to dispute; unquestionable.
The district attorney attempted to present incontrovertible proof of the defendant's guilt.

incorrigible (in-KORE-ij-uh-bul), adjective
Impossible to correct or reform. Very difficult to control or keep in order. If you babysit often, you probably have lots of opportunities to use this word.

*It's premature to call a challenging kindergartener **incorrigible**, but those who had dealt with Katie were greatly tempted to do so.*

incredulous (in-KRE-joo-lus), adjective
Unable or unwilling to believe something. Unconvinced, or demonstrating disbelief. This is a look you've seen often on your parents' faces; now you know what to call it.

*The teenager was **incredulous** when accused of cheating, for he was a good student.*

inculcate (IN-kul-kate), verb
To fix something firmly in someone's mind using frequent and forceful repetition. To teach by means of repetition or instruction. To impress an idea upon someone with urging or earnest example.

*Police use "scared straight" strategies with at-risk youth, **inculcating** them with lessons related to the negative consequences of their actions, and instilling the fear of incarceration.*

inculpate (in-KUL-pate), verb
To incriminate someone or put the blame for something on someone. Blame for a wrongdoing.

*Motive and opportunity are two of the critical factors determined to **inculpate** suspects for murder.*

indefatigable (in-dih-FA-tih-guh-bul), adjective
Never showing signs of getting tired, or of relaxing an effort; unyielding stamina.

*Michael Jordan seemed **indefatigable**, playing as hard in the fourth quarter as he did in the first.*

indolent (IN-duh-lent), adjective
Lazy, lethargic, not showing interest in making an effort, as a way of life. Inactive and unlikely to exert oneself. Also used to describe a disease or condition that is slow to develop or heal, yet causes no pain. "Indolent adolescent" seems a little redundant.
Indolent youths don't participate in athletics or in anything else.

inebriate (ih-NEE-bree-ate), verb
To cause someone to become drunk or intoxicated; to make excited or exhilarated.
Prior to the state championship game, the anticipation and excitement inebriated all of the players.

ineffable (ih-NEH-fuh-bull), adjective
Incapable of being expressed in words; indescribable. To an extreme degree or unbelievable degree. Also describes things or subjects that should not be spoken of.
John Kennedy's ineffable charisma as projected via the first-ever televised debate was credited by some as a reason he won the close 1960 presidential election.

inexorable (ih-NEKS-or-ruh-bul), adjective
Unyielding. Something that is stubborn or unwavering is inexorable. This is a good word to describe the power of a chocolate chip cookie over the average chocoholic.
"The inexorable advance of our troops," the Union general said happily, "will complicate things for Mr. Davis."

inexplicable (ih-nik-SPLIH-kuh-bul), adjective
Incapable of being explained, justified, or interpreted. For someone who is not a chocoholic, the power of chocolate is inexplicable.
Peter's failure to show up for his final exam was inexplicable.

infallible (in-FA-luh-bul), adjective
Incapable of making a mistake. Certain not to fail. Beyond error in religious matters of doctrine or dogma.
Those who believe computers are infallible have never had a software virus.

infer (in-FUR), verb

To conclude something on the basis of evidence or reasoning. To suggest or lead to a conclusion. Too often confused with *imply*, which means to make something understood without expressing it directly.

You can infer from her absence that she does not support the actions of her neighbors to remove the old oak trees.

infrastructure (IN-fruh-struk-chur), noun

The foundation or structure of a system or organization. The large-scale public systems, services, and facilities of a country or region necessary for economic activity. The essential primary components of a system, organization, or structure.

A city's infrastructure influences its potential for future growth and greatness, or decline and failure.

ingratiate (in-GRAY-she-ate), verb

To try to gain someone's favor, especially in order to gain an advantage. Sounds like but not the same as *ingrate*, a person who does not show or express gratitude.

When he first met his fiancée's parents, Chuck tried to ingratiate himself with his future father-in-law.

inherent (in-HARE-unt), adjective

An innate characteristic of something; intrinsic or essential to something. Not to be confused with *inherit*, which means to become an owner of something when someone dies, in accordance with terms of a will.

Dwayne's inherent reluctance to entrust newcomers with tasks of any significance was a major problem for the company.

innate (ih-NATE), adjective

Characteristic or quality possessed at birth; inborn or central to a person.

Lana's ability to do mathematics problems since early childhood seemed innate.

innocuous (ih-NAH-kyoo-wus), adjective
Not intended to cause offense or provoke a strong reaction. Lacking conflict or drama. Harmless, of minimal significance, interest, or prominence.

Teasing is thought to be innocuous, until someone gets angry and fighting begins.

inscrutable (in-SKROO-tuh-bul), adjective
Hard to interpret because something is not expressed obviously. Dense or difficult to understand or to decipher.

The Mona Lisa's inscrutable smile has inspired eclectic emotions and thoughts in those privileged to view the painting.

insipid (in-SIH-pid), adjective
Dull, lacking in vigor and character. Used to describe bland ideas, personalities, or works of art. From the Latin for "without taste."

The film critic seemed to describe most movies as insipid, so readers hoped he was not accurate all the time.

insolent (IN-suh-lent), adjective
Showing aggressive lack of respect; rude and arrogant in speech or behavior or disrespectful.

Many adolescent boys appear insolent, when some are just naturally challenging authority.

insolvent (IN-sulv-ent), adjective
Unable to pay debts. Related to people or businesses that are bankrupt.

It sounds so much nicer to say "I'm insolvent," rather than "I'm broke," but they mean the same.

inspiration (in-spuh-RAY-shun), noun
Something that stimulates creative thoughts and actions, or the making of a work of art. A sudden brilliant idea. Someone or something that inspires somebody. Divine guidance and influence.

Some idiosyncratic artists think procrastination precedes inspiration.

insurgent (in-SUR-junt), noun
Someone who rebels against authority or leadership. Refers especially to those involved in an uprising against a government. Member of a political party who rebels against party leaders or policies.

*The government admitted that some parts of the country were under the control of **insurgents**.*

intercession (IN-ter-SEH-shun), noun
The act of pleading on someone's behalf. The attempt to settle a dispute; mediation of a conflict by acting or speaking in someone's behalf.

*The coach's quick **intercession** stopped the fight before anyone from either team was ejected.*

interpolate (in-TER-puh-layt), verb
To insert something, often unnecessary, between two elements. To add comments or extra words to a written text or conversation, altering or falsifying its meaning. To estimate the value of a mathematical function that lies between known values, usually done by projecting graph points.

*Actuaries use statistics to **interpolate** customers' potential life expectancy, and that's how they figure out how much to charge for an insurance policy.*

intransigence (in-TRAN-sih-jents), noun
A firm, unyielding, or unreasonable refusal to even consider changing a decision or attitude. Being uncompromising, beyond appeal or negotiation. This word might describe your parents when you suggest a new motorcycle for the purposes of transportation.

*The **intransigence** of the union negotiators meant that the strike would continue.*

intrinsic (in-TRIN-zik), adjective
Belonging to something as a basic and essential element. By itself, rather than because of an association or consequences. Essential in nature; fundamental in character.

*The **intrinsic** conflict between good and evil is a constant theme in literature.*

intuition (in-TOO-wih-shun), noun
State of being aware of or knowing something through direct insight without any reasoning. Something believed or known instinctively without tangible evidence. Immediate knowledge of something.

*Martin's **intuition** inspired him to buy an initial public offering of a stock that quickly rose greatly in value.*

inundation (in-nun-DAY-shun), noun
A flood of water. Also, an overwhelming amount of things to deal with.

*The newlyweds returned home to an **inundation** of family and friends who wanted to see them, but they wanted some time alone.*

invective (in-VEK-tiv), noun
Abusive expression, or language used to denounce, attack, or blame someone. Extremely harsh speech or writing.

*Angry over being charged with a foul, the basketball team's best player shouted **invectives** at the referee, and he was immediately ejected from the game.*

irony (eye-roh-nee), noun
The use of words to suggest the opposite of their literal meaning, often used in humor. Something that happens that is not what might be expected, especially when it seems absurd, laughable or coincidental. That you can't iron iron could be called an irony.

*The **irony** was that even as leaders of the former Soviet Union protested American capitalism, Levi jeans were the hottest and most expensive items on Moscow's black market.*

irreverent (ih-REV-runt), adjective
Lacking in respect. Displaying behavior that is disrespectful. A reverend is rarely irreverent.

***Irreverent** comedians often use words that are considered expletives.*

iteration (ih-tuh-RAY-shun), noun
An instance or the act of repeating something. A series of steps that is repeated to get closer to a desired outcome. A different version of something, as in a newer version of a video game.

*After several **iterations**, the chefs found the best recipe for chocolate cheesecake.*

jejune (jih-JOON), adjective

Uninteresting and intellectually undemanding. Dull or lackluster. Can also mean lacking in sophistication or insight. Lacking proper nourishment. Not very fertile.

Many of those taking their first music lessons have jejune dreams of fame, fortune, and standing room only gigs.

jingoism (JIN-go-ih-zuhm), noun

Zealous patriotism, especially in hostility toward other countries. Aggressive and overbearing patriotism; blindly nationalistic.

Jingoism usually manifests at times of war or just prior to war.

Where'd That Word Come From?

Jingoism—A refrain from a British music hall song that urged Great Britain to fight the Russians and prevent them from taking Constantinople goes: "We don't want to fight, yet by Jingo, if we do, we've got the ships, we've got the men, and the money, too." This is the origin of this expression for "chauvinism or excessive patriotism." *Jingo* is a euphemism for "by Jesus" that dates back to the late seventeenth century.

---

jobbery (JAH-buh-ree), noun

The corrupt practice of making private gains from public office. This one's easy to remember: Jobbery is robbery by a politician.

The senator was accused of jobbery by his opponent, yet he was never charged formally.

jocular (JAH-kyoo-lur), adjective

Having a playful, joking disposition. Intended to be funny; made in jest.

Stan's always jocular behavior and attitude was out of place during serious times.

joie de vivre (ZSHWA duh VEEV), noun
Energy and love of life. Originally a French phrase, but now commonly used in English.

The joie de vivre she demonstrated in the most difficult circumstances was an inspiration to everyone around her.

jovial (JOE-vee-uhl), adjective
Cheerful in mood or disposition. Synonymous with *jocular*, and another way to say happy and funny.

Winning that much money on a lottery ticket would certainly put anyone in a jovial mood.

Where'd That Word Come From?

Jovial—Derived from the Latin *jovialis*, of or pertaining to Jupiter or Jove, the chief god of the Romans (equivalent of the Greek god Zeus). Describing a hearty, merry person, it is said to have been first used by British author Gabriel Harvey in about 1590. At least, Thomas Nash claimed Harvey invented the word, along with *conscious*, *extensively*, *idiom*, *notoriety*, and *rascality*—all of which Nash disliked and said would not last.

---

judicious (JOO-di-shus), adjective
Showing wisdom, good sense, or discretion, often with the intention of avoiding trouble or waste.

Since his earlier troubles, Jonah was very judicious whenever he partied with friends.

juggernaut (JUH-guhr-not), noun
A force that is relentlessly destructive and that crushes all obstacles in its way.

The Green Bay Packers of the early 1960s were considered a professional football juggernaut.

junta (HOON-tah), noun
Group of military officers who have taken control of a county following a coup. A small group secretly assembled for a common goal.

During difficult economic times, leaders of young democracies are fearful of military juntas.

jurisdiction (joor-iss-DICK-shun), noun
The authority to enforce laws or pronounce legal judgments; power or authority generally.

Judge Judy's jurisdiction seemed to reach far beyond specific geographic boundaries.

jurist (JOOR-ust), noun
An expert in the science or philosophy of law, especially a judge or legal scholar. Not to be confused with *juror,* who is someone sworn to an oath to serve on a jury.

All Supreme Court justices are jurists and legal scholars beyond question.

jury-rig (JOOR-ee rihg), verb
To build something in a makeshift way, or fit something with makeshift equipment. Despite including the word *jury,* the term has nothing to do with law.

Stranded in the desert, the team had to jury-rig tools and parts to repair the truck when it broke down.

juxtapose (JUK-stuh-pose), verb
To place (or pose) two or more things together, side by side for comparison and contrast, or to suggest a link between them.

Juxtaposed, the pictures of Jay and his son showed an amazing family resemblance.

Kafkaesque (kahf-KAH-esk), adjective
Related to, typical of, or similar to the work of Franz Kafka, a writer whose novels and plays were quite complicated and often disturbing. Overly complex, seemingly pointless, and impersonal. If you use this word, you'll sound smart, especially if you know who Kafka is and if you've read one of his works. How about *The Metamorphosis*?
*Her short story had a very **Kafkaesque** atmosphere, but it still wasn't very good.*

kangaroo court (kan-guh-ROO CORT), noun
An unofficial court that is set up on the spot to deliver a judgment that had already been decided in advance. A situation when someone is prejudged and unable to receive a fair hearing or trial. From history, when those convicted of crimes were sent from Britain to Australia, where this large leaping animal is indigenous.
*Recently, a defense attorney was placed in jail for referring to the proceedings as a **kangaroo court**.*

keepsake (KEEP-sake), noun
A small item or gift kept to evoke memories of something, an event, or someone.
*Before she left for college, Samantha gave her mom the tassel from her high school graduation cap as a **keepsake**.*

kickback (KIHK-bahk), noun
A reaction that is quick and violent, as when a chainsaw bites into metal. Also money received illegally in return for a secret agreement (also usually illegal).
*The contractor was accused of taking **kickbacks** from suppliers who charged excessive prices.*

kinetic (kih-NET-ik), adjective
Pertaining to, caused by, or producing motion. Kinetic energy is the energy associated with the movement of a system or body.
*Alexander Calder is credited for inventing the mobile, a **kinetic** sculpture with hanging pieces that move and flow.*

L

kowtow (kow-TOW) verb
To kneel with forehead touching the ground to worship or show respect. To be extremely submissive to please someone in authority.

Prior to the French Revolution, all citizens would ***kowtow*** *to anyone who was royal, for fear of punishment or death.*

Where'd That Word Come From?

Kowtow—The Chinese *k'-o-t'ou*, spelled in English as *kowtow*, means "know your head"—that is, to kneel and bow before a superior by touching the floor with your forehead. Mandarins required the *k'-o-t'ou* of their "inferiors." Explorers visiting China at the end of the nineteenth century brought back the word. To *kowtow* to someone has come to mean to act in an obsequious and groveling way—that is, doing pretty much everything short of touching your head on the floor.

---

kudos (KOO-dos), noun
Praise, credit, glory, honor or accolades for an achievement. A black belt in judo earns tons of kudos.

*****Kudos*** *were offered to all graduates at the commencement ceremony and during the receptions that followed it.*

laborious (lah-BORE-ee-us), adjective
Requiring a great deal of effort. Showing signs of effort or difficulty, rather than easy, naturalness, or fluency.

Most high school boys find any work, no matter how hard or long it is, to be ***laborious***.

labyrinth (LA-buh-rinth), noun
A maze or maze-like structure. In Greek mythology, the maze designed by Daedalus for King Minos of Crete to confine the Minotaur.

The hallways of the new high school seemed like a ***labyrinth*** *to the new freshmen, and many became lost on their first days.*

laconic (luh-KON-ik), adjective
Using very few words; concise or terse writing or speech.
A laconic politician is hard to find, so if you can identify a candidate who is concise and honest, vote for him or her.

laggard (LAG-urd), noun
Someone who or something that falls behind and does not keep up with others. One who lags behind or loiters. Most often used as a negative description.
It was insensitive and unprofessional of the teacher to refer to those who were falling behind in the difficult mathematics class as laggards.

laissez-faire (leh-zay FARE), noun
The principle that the best economy is one that does not regulate private industry and leaves markets free. Noninterference in the affairs of others; letting others do as they wish.
Ironically, many who believe in economical laissez-faire often support governmental interference in the affairs of other nations.

laity (LAY-uh-tee), noun
Followers of a religion who are not clergy; lay persons. All who are not members of a specific profession.
The laity of the Catholic Church is growing more and more independent and less likely to follow the dictates of the Pope.

lambaste (LAM-baste), verb
To criticize someone or something severely; to reprimand sharply or attack verbally. To beat or whip someone. Originally meant "to beat harshly."
Teenagers are lambasted for staying out past curfew so commonly that it might be called a rite of passage.

languid (LANG-gwid), adjective
Lacking vigor and energy. Listless, indifferent, sluggish, or slow.
Those who are frequently languid may be suffering from some malady or disability.

languish (LANG-gwish), verb

To undergo hardship as a result of being deprived of something, typically independence, attention, or freedom. To decline steadily, becoming less vital, strong, or successful. To long for something being denied.

Famous musicians often languished for years in obscurity before being discovered and catapulted overnight to stardom.

largess (lar-ZHESS), noun

Generous gifts, often in the form of money or favors. The gifts given as a result of someone's generosity. Generosity in spirit or attitude; a generous nature. Largish gifts reveal largess of givers.

The largess of wealthy individuals is often surprising, for some believe them to be less than generous.

lax (LAKS), adjective

Not strict, tight, or tense; not easily controlled. Lacking attention to detail.

After the investigation it was concluded that Bob had been lax when inspecting the bridge for structural faults.

learned (LUR-nid), adjective

Well-educated and very knowledgeable. Describes behavior or knowledge that is acquired through training.

The learned scholar was greatly respected among those who studied anthropology.

lector (LEK-tohr), noun

A university lecturer or one who reads passages from the Bible to a congregation at a service, or during a meal.

The lector stood very formally, in academic regalia, ready to deliver the annual lecture on abstinence and temperance.

LED (EL-ee-dee), noun

Acronym for "light-emitting diode." A semiconductor that emits light when a current passes through it. Used as indicators on electronic devices.

Once a novelty, LED displays in automobiles are now standard equipment.

left-brain (LEFT-brayn), adjective
Relating to or involving skills or knowledge that is analytical or linguistic, believed associated with the left half of the cerebrum.

Left-brain thought was required for mathematics exams, while right-brain effort was required for the music appreciation tests.

leftism (LEF-tih-zum), noun
The principles of the Left; liberal, socialist, or communist political and social movements or reform.

It seems that conservatives are always accusing those who disagree with them of leftism.

legacy (LE-guh-see), noun
Money or property that is left someone in a will. Something handed down that remains in a family from a previous generation or time.

The classic Model T Ford is a legacy passed down within the family from its original owner, great-grandfather Joseph.

leniency (LEE-nee-uhnt-see), noun
Punishment, judgment, or action that is not too severe. Personal quality of being lenient and forgiving; mercy.

The suspect admitted his guilt, hoping that it would lead to leniency at sentencing.

lethargic (luh-THAR-jik), adjective
Sluggish; inactive to such a degree as to resemble sleep or unconsciousness. A lethargic person is difficult to rouse to action.

After many long hours of work, Pat and Corey were lethargic but still unable to accept the necessity of calling it a night.

leviathan (lih-VIE-uh-thun), noun
Large beast or sea monster, originally from the Bible. Something extremely large and powerful in comparison to others of its kind. A whale or other large sea animal.

Cruise ships are getting bigger and bigger, appearing as leviathans as they move across the ocean's horizon.

levity (LEH-vuh-tee), noun
Remarks or behavior intended to be amusing, usually out of keeping with a serious situation. Light-hearted comments or behavior.

Sometimes **levity** *is a way of relieving the anxiety of a crisis situation.*

lexicon (LEK-suh-kon), noun
A reference book composed of an alphabetized listing of words and meaning, especially one dealing with a specific, narrowly defined audience or ancient language. Lexicon can also mean the entire collection of words associated with a specific discipline or group.

The **lexicon** *of rap music seems a different language to many parents, but it is an adaptation of street English.*

liaison (LEE-uh-ZON), noun
An exchange of information among separate groups or individuals. A person responsible for maintaining communication between one group and another. An intimate, romantic relationship between unmarried people.

Nurse Sheffield was appointed to be the pediatric department's **liaison** *with the transplant unit.*

libation (lie-BAY-shun), noun
An alcoholic beverage offered or accepted in celebration. Originally, pouring out of liquid such as wine or oil as a sacrifice to a god or in honor of the dead in a religious ceremony. In other words, a fancy way of saying "shot" or "chug."

Some think it is adult to consume a **libation** *every evening, and others think it quite immature.*

liberalism (LIH-buh-rah-LIH-zum), noun
A theory found in both economics and in politics. In economics, it emphasizes the freedom of the individual consumer and of the market. In politics, it is founded on the protection of civil liberties and on a belief in progress toward a better society.

Economic and social **liberalism** *are not at all the same things.*

libido (lih-BEE-doh), noun
Sexual drive. The psychic and emotional energy associated with basic human instincts, including the sex drive.
*The **libido** of adolescents is sometimes difficult to understand and to control.*

licentious (lie-SEN-shus), adjective
Lacking restraint when it comes to pursuing desires aggressively and selfishly, including those of a sexual nature. Unchecked by morality.
*Wealth and power are not acceptable excuses for **licentious** behavior.*

litany (LIH-tuh-nee), noun
A responsive prayer marked by much repetition. A long and repetitious list of things such as complaints or problems.
*Whenever his father got angry, Brad had to listen to the entire **litany** of his faults.*

literate (LIH-tuh-rut), adjective
Having the ability to read and write. Well educated; skilled and cultured, particularly in regard to literature and writing. A good understanding of a particular subject.
***Literate** students are a teacher's delight.*

litigious (lih-TIH-jus), adjective
Overly inclined to quarrel and argue. Tending to engage in lawsuits. Related to litigation.
*It's difficult to say how much attorneys have promoted the **litigious** trends apparent today, or whether they are the responsibility of society in general.*

livid (LIH-vid), adjective
Discolored, as in a bruise. Also a change from normal coloring, whether from a lack of it or an excess. Very angry.
*Justin's father was **livid** when he found out his son was buying alcohol with a counterfeit driver's license.*

L

lobby (LAH-bee) verb

To attempt to persuade a political representative or influential person to support a fight, particular cause, or specific vote. Guess how this activity got its name? From where it usually happened—in the lobby prior to a vote.

*The firearms **lobby** in the United States is so strong that it has always managed to defeat most gun control legislation.*

locution (loe-KYOO-shun), noun

A phrase or expression typically used by a group of people. The way someone or some groups speak; style of speaking. Also a particular word, expression, or phrase.

*Because Jacqueline was unfamiliar with this group's particular **locutions**, much of what they said was odd to her.*

loquacious (loe-KWAY-shuss), adjective

Tending to talk a great deal. Extremely talkative. Someone prone to nervous chatter could be said to be loquacious.

*It was difficult to tell whether Julia's **loquacious** behavior was caused by nervousness, or whether she always spoke incessantly.*

lucid (LOO-sid), adjective

Clear and easily understood; intelligible. Rational and mentally clear. Also means filled with light.

*After the accident Alex was **lucid** for a while, but he soon lost consciousness and his friends feared the worst.*

ludicrous (LOO-dih-kruss), adjective

Utterly ridiculous, absurd, incongruous, implausible, impractical, or unsuitable.

*It's **ludicrous** to expect that teenagers will behave all of the time, in all circumstances.*

lugubrious (loo-GOO-bree-us), adjective
Extremely sad or gloomy. Lugubrious describes someone who is mournful to an inappropriate degree. Realizing that you're ludicrous may make you lugubrious.

*It was too bad that the football team lost in the season finale, but it doesn't really justify going around with a **lugubrious** expression for weeks afterward.*

luminary (LOO-muh-nair-ee), noun
An eminent or famous person. A glowing object, especially a celestial body that emits light.

*Crowds at the Academy Awards hope to see a **luminary** arriving for the ceremonies.*

luminescent (LOOM-in-ess-sent), adjective
Emitting light produced by means other than heat.

***Luminescent** paint that glows under special lights was popular in the 1960s.*

lurid (LOOR-id), adjective
Gruesome or sensationalistic. Causing horror, lust, shock, or disgust. Lurid movies are a lure to certain viewers, especially men in their late teens and early twenties.

*The **lurid** details of the prison abuses were discussed widely, but few pictures were shown on television.*

lustrous (LUS-truss), adjective
Radiant; shining; having a sheen or glow. Brilliant, outstanding, or exceptional.

*Gloria's **lustrous** performance earned her critical acclaim and the recognition of her thespian peers.*

macabre (muh-KAHB), adjective
Using death as subject, as in movies, books, or conversation; focused on the morbid and grisly. Horrifying.

***Macabre** movies are very popular with almost all teen viewers, male and female.*

M

machismo (mah-CHEEZ-mow), noun
Exaggerated sense or display of masculinity. An emphasis on qualities typically considered male, such as strength, courage, aggressiveness, and lack of emotion.
Driving a motorcycle is for some a demonstration of machismo.

macroeconomics (MA-kroe-eh-kuh-NAH-micks), noun
The study of economics that focuses on the big picture, especially the systems that make up a national or international economy. Also, a study of the ways different parts of the overall system are connected.
Those studying macroeconomics learn about supply and demand and other factors that impact the nation's economy.

maestro (MYS-troe), noun
An expert in an art, especially music; a conductor, composer, or music teacher of high regard.
The violin students eagerly awaited the maestro, who was teaching them a complex arrangement that he would then conduct at their spring performance.

magnanimous (mag-NAH-nuh-mus), adjective
Very generous, kind, or forgiving. Has nothing to do with volcanoes or magma.
In a magnanimous gesture, the wealthy alumnus, who had once been suspended for bad grades, donated $10,000,000 to his alma mater.

mainframe (MANE-FRAYM), noun
Fast powerful computer with a large storage capacity that has a number of terminals for individual users connected to it.
As personal computers became faster and cheaper, the university had less need (and less room) for its mainframes.

malady (MA-luh-dee), noun
A disease or illness of the body or the mind. An unhealthy, problematic condition that causes discomfort and requires a remedy.
New doctors sometimes fear that an undiagnosed malady will cause a patient's death.

malaise (MUH-layze), noun
General feeling of illness or sickness. Vague sense of worry, discontent, or dissatisfaction and the bad feelings that come with it. Not to be confused with Malaysian, a person from Malaysia.

*Doctors could not diagnose any particular disorder, yet Page still suffered from a **malaise** she could not overcome.*

malapropism (MA-la-prah-pi-zuhm), noun
Misuse of a word through confusion with another word that sounds similar, especially with a humorous or ridiculous effect. "The physical year ends in June" is a malapropism for "The fiscal year ends in June."

*Those who confuse and misuse words make many a **malapropism**.*

malevolent (muh-LEH-vuh-lent), adjective
Demonstrating or having a desire to harm others. Malicious and viciously ill-willed.

*The two boxers stood toe to toe, each with a **malevolent** glare focused on the other.*

malign (MUH-line), verb
To say or write bad, unpleasant, and disparaging things that are potentially damaging and may not be true.

*Stuart's editorial clearly sought to **malign** the reputation of fraternities, for he thought they should be eliminated.*

manic (MA-nik), adjective
Relating to or affective by mania; extremely or excessively happy, busy, active, agitated, of high excitement or nervous energy.

*Chaperones are suspicious of **manic** behavior in teens at dances, for sometimes it means they have been drinking.*

manifesto (ma-nuh-FES-toh), noun
A public, written declaration of principles, policies, and objectives. Often issued by a political movement, candidate, or leader.

*The Communist **Manifesto**, by Karl Marx and Friedrich Engels, inspired a political and economic movement that lasted decades yet ultimately proved finite.*

marginal (MARJ-nul), adjective

Very small in scale or importance, as written in a margin. Not of central importance or relevance. Close to the lowest acceptable value or limit. In business terms, barely able to cover the costs of production when sold or when producing goods for sale; not truly profitable.

*Trudy studied harder, but there was only **marginal** improvement in her grades, so she agreed to get a tutor.*

martyr (MAR-tuhr), noun

Someone who chooses to die rather than deny religious, political, or other strong beliefs. Someone who suffers or sacrifices to advance a cause or principle. Someone who experiences great and constant pain. Someone who complains a great deal to solicit sympathy.

*Seeking to become **martyrs**, kamikaze pilots of World War II flew their explosive-laden planes into enemy targets.*

Where'd That Word Come From?

Martyr—Derived from the Greek word for "witness," early Christians used this word to honor those who preferred to accept the penalty of death rather than renounce their faith.

---

masticate (MASS-tuh-kate), verb

To grind, pulverize, or chew using the teeth and jaws. To grind or crush something until it turns to pulp.

*Grandpa, always an extravagant speaker, referred to his dentures as his "**masticating** companions."*

matriculate (muh-TRIH-kyoo-late), verb

To enroll as a member of a specific group or body, especially a college or university. Don't confuse with *masticate*, which means to chew.

*After all of the admissions challenges and decisions, it was a relief for Kim to finally **matriculate** to the University of Rochester.*

matrix (MAY-ricks), noun
A situation, circumstance, or substance that allows for origin, development, or growth of something. A substance within which something is embedded or enclosed. It's more than just a movie title!
*Necessity often seems to be the **matrix** of innovative thinking.*

mea culpa (MAY-ah CUL-pah), noun
An admission of one's own guilt. Formal apology or acknowledgement of responsibility. Latin for "on my head."
*Bradley offered a **mea culpa** after he lost the tickets to the concert.*

mellifluous (meh-LIH-floo-wus), adjective
Pleasant and soothing to listen to; sweet or rich in tone. Filled with a smooth, sweet substance.
*The voices of passionate preachers are **mellifluous**, making the congregation feel as if they were singing their sermons.*

mendacity (men-DA-suh-tee), noun
Deliberate untruthfulness; a lie or falsehood. A very fancy, yet powerful way to say "a lie."
*Even after he was caught red-handed, Brian still thought his **mendacities** would be believed.*

mentor (MEN-tor), noun
Someone, often older or more experienced, who is trusted to advise, counsel, and teach another person who is younger or less experienced.
*Each freshman was assigned a **mentor** from the senior class who was meant to provide help in adjusting to campus life more quickly and easily.*

mercurial (mer-KYOOR-ee-uhl), adjective
Lively, witty, fast-talking, hard to catch, and likely to do the unexpected. Caused by or containing mercury. Originally, relating to the god Mercury or born under that planet.
*His **mercurial** ways made Matthew hard to understand and even harder to get to know.*

M

metamorphosis (meh-tuh-MORE-fuh-sus), noun
A complete or significant change of the body, appearance, character, or condition. A transformation caused by supposed magic or supernatural powers. Franz Kafka's famous story, *The Metamorphosis*, describes a man who changes into a cockroach.

*The caterpillar's **metamorphosis** into a butterfly is one of nature's most amazing transformations.*

Where'd That Word Come From?
Mentor—Mentor, in Greek mythology, was the friend of Odysseus who took charge of his household when the hero of Homer's *Odyssey* went off to war. When problems arose, Pallas Athena descended from heaven to inhabit Mentor's body and, through him, to give good advice to Odysseus's son Telemachus. Mentor has since meant an adviser, teacher, or coach.

microcosm (MY-kruh-kah-zum), noun
A model that represents a larger system; literally, a miniature world.

The characters and settings of the novel The Great Gatsby *show us the social issues and concerns of the 1920s in **microcosm**.*

micromanage (MY-crow-ma-nij), verb
To manage a business or organization by paying extreme (and usually excessive) attention to small details. To retain personal responsibility for overseeing all details of an organization or project.

*Some who **micromanage** contribute a great deal, yet others do more harm than good.*

migratory (MY-gruh-toar-ee), adjective
Moving as part of a bird, fish, or animal population from one region to another every year. Relating to movement of people or animals from one place to another. Tending to wander from one region to another without settling down for any length of time.

***Migratory** birds are good indicators of seasonal changes.*

milestone (MYEL-stone), noun

A stone or other marker on a road that indicates the number of miles to a given place. A significant or important event in someone's life or in the history of a country, a family, or an organization.

The bar mitzvah celebrated by Jewish young men when they are thirteen is a milestone for the entire family.

milieu (meel-YUH), noun

The surroundings or environment that someone lives in and is influenced by. Describing the circumstances or environment around a person or thing. A fancy way of saying "what's around you."

The principal thought a positive and friendly milieu would benefit the new students, so she approved some renovations to the cafeteria.

mimic (MIH-mik), verb

To imitate someone; to copy someone's voice, gestures, or appearance. To resemble someone or something to be a deliberate copy.

Many popular comedians tell stories of how they used to mimic teachers, friends, and family when they were young.

mire (MYRE), verb

To get stuck in mud, either yourself or something else. To make something muddy or dirty. To involve or entangle someone or something in difficulty. Often a part of the phrase "muck and mire."

Many college students become mired in credit card debt soon after commencement.

misanthrope (MIH-sun-thrope), noun

Someone who hates mankind in general, or dislikes and distrusts other people, avoiding them. A person with contempt for the human race.

Scrooge is perhaps literature's most famous misanthrope, so much so that his name is now synonymous with that word.

misconstrue (miss-kun-STROO), verb

To understand or interpret incorrectly; misinterpret. To make an error of analysis.

Many of the candidate's statements were **misconstrued**, *and she lost the election by a landslide.*

mishmash (MISH-mash), noun

A disorderly collection or confused mixture of things; a jumble. Not to be confused with *mismatch*, which means a pairing or combination of people or things that are incompatible or ill-suited.

When young children dress themselves, parents are not surprised to find they choose a **mishmash** *of colors and styles.*

misogyny (muh-SAH-juh-nee), noun

Hatred of women. A bitter contempt for all women.

Trying to drown his sorrows after breaking up with his girlfriend, Jim's inebriated ranting sounded much like **misogyny**.

mitigate (MIH-tuh-gate), verb

To make an offense or crime less serious or more excusable. To lessen harshness, severity, violence, impact, or degree.

By turning state's evidence and testifying against the suspected embezzlers, Mark hoped to **mitigate** *his own guilt and contributions to the shady business deal.*

mitosis (my-TOH-sus), noun

The process by which a cell divides into two cells, with each having the same number of chromosomes as the original cell.

Mitosis is fundamental to the subject of biology, and students must understand it if they plan to learn about genetics.

mnemonic (nih-MAH-nik), noun

Any device, like a rhyme or phrase, meant to make memorizing easier. It could be as simple as tying a string on one's finger, or using an acronym, anagram, or sentence.

ROY G. BIV is a **mnemonic** *used to remember all of the colors in the rainbow: red, orange, yellow, green, blue, indigo, and violet.*

modicum (MAH-dih-kum), noun
A small amount, especially of something abstract such as a quality or characteristic.

*The police had hoped to hear at least a **modicum** of truth as they questioned the suspects about the robbery.*

moiety (MOY-ih-tee) noun
Either of the two parts, not necessarily equal, into which something is divided. A part, portion, or share. Either of two kinship groups divided by and defined by descent, that together make up a tribe or society.

*The hungry fishermen divided their small catch, and each ate his **moiety** with great appreciation.*

mollify (MAH-luh-fie), verb
To calm or soothe someone who is upset; to appease someone's anger. To lessen the impact of.

*The father's attempts to **mollify** his two arguing daughters were unsuccessful, so the screaming and crying went on for hours.*

monograph (MAH-nuh-graff), noun
A scholarly academic-focused article, paper, or essay on a single topic. It is easy to imagine most monographs being read in a monotone.

*Professor Smith's **monograph** on religious philosophy was his first serious academic publication since his doctoral thesis.*

moribund (MORE-uh-bund), adjective
Nearly dead. Having lost all sense of purpose or vitality. Becoming obsolete or about to die. Literally, "bound toward death."

*It was sad to visit Grandpa after his stroke, for this once energetic man lay **moribund** in bed, hardly speaking or moving.*

morose (muh-ROCE), adjective
Having a withdrawn or gloomy personality; melancholy or sullen.

*As the shells landed closer, the enemy soldiers grew more **morose** as their chances of survival lessened.*

mortal (MORE-tuhl), adjective

Certain to die eventually. Being the cause of death, as in a mortal wound or injury. Extreme, as in a mortal enemy, or intensely felt, as in mortal terror.

Teenagers who often cross the street without looking seem unaware that they are mortal.

mortgage (MOR-gaj), noun

Agreement that lets someone borrow money against a valuable piece of property, such as a house, giving the lender the right to seize the property if the loan is not paid. A written contract between borrower and lender, or the total amount of money lent. Also the amount paid by the borrower, usually every month, until the sum is repaid.

If they could get a mortgage, the newlyweds would be able to buy their dream house.

mortification (MORE-tuh-fuh-KAY-shun), noun

To control or put an end to bodily desires by means of abstinence from pleasure and self-inflicted pain. Deep shame and humiliation caused by a blow to one's pride.

A deep sense of mortification overcame the congregation when they learned how little had been pledged for the new rectory.

motley (MOT-lee), adjective

Composed of people or things that are very different and don't seem to belong together. Made of different colors.

As a caring Little League coach, Paul was highly motivated to turn his motley group of kids into a confident team.

multifaceted (mul-tee-FA-sih-tid), adjective

With many different talents, qualities, or features; possessing many facets, dimensions, or cut surfaces.

Spencer Tracy was a multifaceted actor, equally proficient at drama or comedy.

mundane (mun-DANE), adjective

Commonplace, boring; ordinary or everyday. Relating to or pertaining to concerns of the workaday world.

*After visiting Stephanie at college, her parents were surprised at how **mundane** the life of this high school partier had become.*

myopia (mye-OH-pee-uh), noun

A common condition that causes an inability to see things clearly from far away; nearsightedness. To lack foresight or long-term planning.

*After the strategic planning meeting, it became evident that the sales team suffered from **myopia** and could not see their manager's vision for success.*

myriad (MEER-ee-ud), adjective

Too great a number to be counted; innumerable. Made of many different elements.

*Elaine's **myriad** talents were all used in her new job directing the all-school musical.*

Where'd That Word Come From?

Myriad—Before the idea of a million was introduced in about the twelfth century, the largest number word was *myriad*, which derives from a Greek word meaning countless, infinite, and was also the Greek word for 10,000. Today, *myriad* is used chiefly to mean countless or innumerable.

You're now halfway through with the list. What do you think? A good way to study up on your new words is to pick one that starts with each letter, A through M, and make a vocabulary list for next week. Then use the words from your list in speech or writing. You can't lose!

Read on, from N through Z, and choose another list of thirteen words for the following week. Do this again and again, and week by week your vocabulary and word power will grow. It's easy; you'll see.

nanosecond (NA-noh-seh-kund), noun
One billionth of a second. Informally, the shortest conceivable period of time. Nay, no second is shorter than a nanosecond.

*It just takes a **nanosecond** for a car accident to happen, so please be focused and careful.*

nanotechnology (NA-noh-tek-NAH-nuh-jee), noun
The ability to manipulate materials on a very small scale, with the goal of building microscopic objects such as machinery. The science of building devices, such as electronic circuits, from individual atoms and molecules.

*It is believed that someday **nanotechnology** will make organ transplantation unnecessary.*

narcissism (NAHR-suh-SIH-zum), noun
Excessive self-admiration and self-centeredness; being possessed by self-love. In medicine, a personality disorder characterized by an overestimation of one's appearance and abilities, and an excessive need for admiration.

***Narcissism** goes well beyond confidence and positive thought; it's quite obvious and disturbing.*

narcolepsy (NAHR-kuh-lehp-see), noun
A disorder characterized by frequent, brief, and uncontrollable bouts of deep sleep.

*While stories about people with **narcolepsy** can be quite funny, the disorder is truly nothing to laugh at.*

narrative (NAR-uh-tiv), noun
Story or account of a sequence of events, presented in the order in which they happened. The art of telling a story or giving a vivid account of something. The portion of a literary work concerned with telling a story.

*The art of the **narrative** is a writing talent that must be nurtured.*

nascent (NA-sunt), adjective
Emerging. Refers to the early stages of coming into existence.

*After the revolution, the **nascent** republic had few if any established democratic traditions, so much work needed to be done.*

NASDAQ (NAA-zdack), acronym

An acronym for "National Association of Securities Dealers Automated Quotation System," a collection of publicly traded stocks that includes a lot of high-tech companies. The electronic communications system that links all over-the-counter securities dealers to form a national market.

*Each day economists analyze **NASDAQ** trading to determine the nature of the market.*

nationalism (NASH-nuh-lizum), noun

Proud loyalty and devotion to a nation; in particular, excessive devotion to a nation and belief it is superior to all others. The desire to achieve independence, particularly by a country under foreign control.

***Nationalism** can be positive when celebrating good, but too often it is an excuse for terrorism and harm.*

NATO (NAY-toe), acronym

An acronym for "North Atlantic Treaty Organization," an international organization established after World War II to promote mutual defense and collective security for the United States and Western Europe.

*Since the fall of the Soviet Union, **NATO** has expanded dramatically to include nations that were once considered foes.*

natty (NA-tee), adjective

Neat and fashionable appearance or dress. A natty dresser would never wear clothes that looked ratty.

*Jayson's **natty** attire was always a welcome sight, especially in comparison to those of his friends who didn't seem to care about their appearance.*

natural selection (NA-chu-rul suh-leck-shun), noun

A theory developed by Charles Darwin to explain the evolution of species, also known as "survival of the fittest." The organisms best suited to survive in a particular environment reproduce in greater numbers than others that are less well suited, thus creating future generations of better-adapted offspring.

*Eventually, **natural selection** survived as the accepted theory, yet it remains controversial to those who accept creationism.*

navigable (NA-vih-guh-bull), adjective
Passable by ship or boat; waters deep and wide enough to allow vessels to pass. Able to be steered or controlled.
   Prior to backing out of the crammed parking lot, Dennis first determined that it was navigable.

naysayer (NAY-say-er), noun
Someone who votes no or who speaks against something. Naysayer Jay says "No," "Never," and "Nay" every day.
   She was always so negative that it became easy to call her a naysayer.

nebulous (NEH-byoo-luss), adjective
Unclear, vague, cloudy, or hazy. Relating to or resembling a nebula (a cloud of dust or gas in interstellar space).
   Some students thought the professor's lectures were too nebulous, so they depended upon the textbook to study for exams.

necromancy (NEH-kruh-man-see), noun
The practice of attempting to communicate with the spirits of the dead in order to predict or influence the future. Witchcraft or sorcery in general.
   Necromancy seems impossible, yet many who want so much to communicate with dead loved ones, and who hope to foretell the future, still believe.

ne'er-do-well (NERR-due-wel), noun
A lazy and irresponsible person. You will do well to ne'er get called this word.
   Lindsay's parents thought her fiancé was a ne'er-do-well, and they tried to tell her so.

nefarious (nih-FAR-ee-us), adjective
Utterly immoral, wicked, unjust, or evil.
   The documents were classified as Top Secret for fear that the information they contained could be used for nefarious acts.

negligent (NEH-gluh-jent), adjective
Habitually careless or irresponsible. Guilty of failing to provide a proper or reasonable level of care.

*Investigators deemed that the nursing home staff had not been **negligent** and thus was not responsible for the accident.*

nemesis (NEH-muh-sus), noun
A bitter enemy, especially one who seems unbeatable. An opponent motivated by revenge; one who will stop at nothing to settle a score or inflict punishment.

*Although he fought many other criminals, Batman's **nemesis** was truly the Joker.*

Where'd That Word Come From?

Nemesis—Nemesis was the Greek goddess of justice or revenge, and her name comes from the Greek for vengeance. Thus, *nemesis* means anyone who avenges or punishes.

neophyte (NEE-uh-fite), noun
A beginner or novice at some task or endeavor. Someone who has recently converted or who has recently joined a religious order but has not yet taken vows to join an order. A veteran boxer might be glad to fight a neophyte.

*Freshmen are truly **neophytes** to college, but they manage to adjust and learn very quickly.*

nepotism (NEH-puh-tih-zum), noun
Favoritism shown by someone in power to relatives and friends in professional matters, especially when appointing them to good positions.

*When senior managers all share the last name of a company's founder, it's unusual if no one is accused of **nepotism**.*

N

netiquette (NET-uh-kit), noun
A set of rules for communicating properly in the electronic communication environment known as the World Wide Web, most often when using e-mail or instant message capabilities.

There should be a class in **netiquette**, *but it would most likely be an online course.*

neural (NUR-ul) adjective
Related to or located in a nerve or the nervous system.

When studying biology, the students were very interested in learning about **neural** *anatomy and connections.*

newbie (NUE-bee), noun
A new user of the Internet, or someone new to any circumstance, organization, or institution.

*Those planning the orientation session thought the term "***newbie***" was appropriate, so it became the theme for the program.*

nexus (NEK-sus), noun
A connection or link; also a group or series of connected people or things. The center or focus. If you've ever been hit in the solar plexus, you know it's the nexus of your ability to breathe.

For many, a shared love of sports is the **nexus** *of their friendship and the inspiration for many conversations.*

nihilism (NIE-uh-lih-zum), noun
The belief that life is pointless and human values worthless. A belief that there is no objective basis for truth, or a belief that all authority is corrupt and must be destroyed to build a just society. The word *annihilate* comes from the same roots, meaning "nothing."

Some believe that Henry David Thoreau, who wrote Walden, *recounting his life celebrating nature and his ability to live independent of society, was an advocate of* **nihilism**.

nitty-gritty (NIH-tee-GRIH-tee), noun
The basic and most important details of something. The thing or approach that is most practical, direct, and down to earth.

*The coach believed wins were a result of paying attention to the **nitty-gritty**, so he always began practice with rudimentary drills.*

noblesse oblige (noh-BLESS oh-BLEEZH), noun
The idea that people born to nobility or upper classes must behave generously toward those less privileged. From the French for "nobility obliges."

*Many of the most famous foundations, named for the wealthiest families, like Carnegie and Rockefeller, were founded on the principle of **noblesse oblige**.*

nocturnal (nahk-TUR-nal), adjective
Occurring at night, in the dark, active during the night. The antonym of *diurnal,* which describes things that happen during the day.

*Once puberty kicks in, it seems that teenagers turn into members of a **nocturnal** species.*

nomad (NOH-mad), noun
Member of a group that moves from place to place, in search of pasture, food, or water. Someone who wanders from one place to another.

*The player, who was just traded to his third team in one season, seemed like a **nomad**.*

nom de plume (nahm duh PLOOM), noun
Pseudonym; the name used by a writer instead of his or her real name. French for "pen name."

*Authors who write romance novels often use a **nom de plume**, for they are a bit embarrassed to be associated with this genre.*

nomenclature (NOH-mun-klay-chur), noun
Name or designation; the act of naming. A system of names for purposes of organization. A system of names created to describe a new scientific or artistic discipline. The nomenclature of the Internet includes terms like "pop-up," "hyperlink," and "bandwidth."

*Upon entering graduate school, Mark realized that he had to learn an entire new **nomenclature** if he was to succeed.*

nostalgia (NAH-stahl-juh), noun
Mixed feeling of happiness, sadness, and longing when recalling persons, places, or events of the past. Something intended to arouse feelings associated with the past. A longing for home or family when away.

*Buying and selling items that inspire **nostalgia** has become a very lucrative business.*

notarize (NOH-tuh-rize), verb
To certify something, like a signature on a legal document, and verify to its authenticity. To certify or attest to the validity of a signature on a document as a notary public.

*Paralegals who are also notaries might **notarize** hundreds of documents each week.*

nouveau riche (NOO-voh REESH), noun
A class of people whose extreme wealth has been recently earned, often a former member of a lower or middle class who ostentatiously displays newly acquired trappings of wealth. Also a member of this class.

*Anyone who disdains the **nouveau riche** must hate the way these people just keep smiling—all the way to the bank.*

noxious (NOK-shuss), adjective
Harmful to life or health; poisonous. Likely to cause moral or spiritual harm; corrupting or debilitating influence. As a teenager, you encounter many things that smell this way. Think locker room, sweat socks, or a long-forgotten tuna sandwich.

*The **noxious** gas was odorless and almost invisible, so it was stored very carefully.*

nuance (NOO-ahnts), noun
A very slight difference in meaning, tone, color, or feeling. Awareness or ability to express subtle shades, meanings, and feelings, as in an artist or performer.

*Jim's ability to see the **nuances** in certain photographs made him an exceptional magazine editor.*

null (NUHL), adjective
Having no legal validity; of no value or importance. Amounting to nothing in terms of context or character. At the level of zero or nothing.
The judge ruled that, in the context of this trial, all of the attorney's objections were null.

nullify (NUH-luh-fie), verb
To make something legally invalid or ineffective; to cancel something out.
Once the deadline passed, without payment being made, Jane could nullify the contract with a simple phone call.

numismatist (noo-miz-muh-tist), noun
Someone who studies or collects coins, paper money, or medals.
I guess it takes money to become a numismatist.

nuptial (NUP-shul), adjective
Related to marriage or weddings.
Renting a tuxedo always seemed nuptial to Stephen, even if he was just doing so for a formal dance.

obesity (oh-BEE-suh-tee), noun
A condition of extreme excess body fat. Technically, a body weight that is 20 percent or more higher than recommended for that person's height.
Obesity is becoming a serious issue for America's youth.

obfuscate (OB-fuss-kate), verb
To make something unclear or obscure, especially unnecessarily complicated; to muddy or confuse an issue. To make something dark or hard to see.
When caught doing wrong, some teens obfuscate their explanation of events, hoping parents won't quite understand.

objet d'art (OB-zhay dahr), noun
An article that has artistic value. French for "object of art."
Phillip thought of his purchase at the garage sale as an objet d'art, but others thought it a garish piece of junk.

oblique (oh-BLEEK), adjective

Not straightforward or direct; indirect and unclear. In mathematics, sloping or adjoining at an angle that is not a right angle; not perpendicular nor parallel.

Professor Blake's description of the relationship between the two novels was so **oblique** *that few students comprehended.*

oblivion (uh-BLIH-vee-un), noun

The state of being utterly forgotten. Complete forgetfulness; utter lack of awareness of one's surroundings.

For a time it was as if roller-skating had been relegated to **oblivion**, *and then in-line skates became popular.*

obsequious (ub-SEE-kwee-uss), adjective

Excessively eager to please or to obey all instructions. Compliant and servile to superiors, in order to curry favor.

For some, it is difficult to distinguish **obsequious** *behavior from sincere and excellent customer service.*

obsolescent (ob-suh-LESS-unt), adjective

Having fallen into a state of disuse as a result of replacement by something new; in short, becoming obsolete. Adolescence becomes obsolescent—or should—as soon as your teen years are behind you.

Many think the piano was made **obsolescent** *by the electronic keyboard, but not everyone agrees.*

obstinate (OB-stih-nut), adjective

Determined not to agree with other people's wishes or accept their suspicions. Unwilling to change or give up an idea or attitude despite obstacles. Difficult to control, get rid of, solve or cure. Not to be confused with *abstinent,* which describes restraint over desires, such as for sex or alcohol.

Arthur was **obstinate** *in his claim that he did not cheat on the exam, so he agreed to a formal review of the case.*

O

obtrusive (ob-TROO-suhv), adjective
Tending to force one's presence or opinions on others. Highly noticeable, often with a bad or unwelcome effect.

James' Uncle Herbert was quite obtrusive, and, frankly, unwelcome at almost all family events.

obtuse (ob-TOOS), adjective
Slow in understanding or perceiving something; with poor powers of intellect or perceptions. In mathematics, describes an angle of greater than 90 degrees and less than 180 degrees. A word that could be used as a fancy description of a few of your friends, no doubt.

Bob was called obtuse for not quite understanding the basics of algebra, but many others find this form of mathematics challenging as well.

obviate (OB-vee-ate), verb
To make something unnecessary, avoiding potential difficulty by acting in anticipation prior to a problem's arising.

It was hoped that constant review of emergency procedures would obviate any need for evacuation at the nuclear plant.

OCD (OH-see-dee), acronym
Acronym for "obsessive-compulsive disorder": a psychological condition characterized by uncontrolled repeated behaviors, such as hand-washing.

Her friends thought she was exhibiting the telltale signs of OCD, but Elaine just thought it appropriate to check her makeup regularly.

odious (OH-dee-us), adjective
Inspiring hatred, contempt, or disgust; abhorrent.

Racial prejudice was once accepted in certain parts of the country, but it is now odious to nearly all Americans.

odoriferous (oh-duh-RIH-fuh-russ), adjective
Having or diffusing a strong odor. Can also refer to actions that are immoral or offensive. Hey, it beats saying "you stink."

While few agreed on whether it was in a good or bad way, everyone thought the candle shop quite odoriferous.

odyssey (AH-duh-see), noun

A long journey; a series of travels, adventures, or dangerous travails. Derives from Homer's epic poem, the *Odyssey*, which describes such a grand journey undertaken by the character Odysseus.

*High school for almost all students is an **odyssey** from childhood to young adulthood, full of many unexpected challenges.*

officiate (uh-FIH-shee-ate), verb

To preside in an official capacity, especially at a particular ceremony.

*It was agreed that Judge Jerome would **officiate** at the wedding.*

old-school (OHLD skool), adjective

Adhering to traditional or old-fashioned values and practices. Yes, it's a movie title as well.

*Stephen's parents were considered **old-school** because they insisted on his having a midnight curfew.*

olfaction (ahl-FAK-shun), noun

The sense of smell. The action of smelling something.

*The lacrosse coaches sometimes dreamed of temporarily suspending their **olfaction**, particularly in the locker room after games.*

oligarchy (AH-luh-gar-kee), noun

A small group that governs a nation, or controls an organization. Government by a few, especially by a small faction of persons or families. Depending on the kind of high school you attend, the oligarchy might be composed of beautiful people, jocks, or super brains.

*Historically, those who were displeased with an aristocracy have called it **oligarchy**, and fought for democracy.*

Olympian (oh-LIHM-pee-un), adjective

Extraordinarily great or demanding, befitting an Olympic athlete. Superior or grand, above everyday events, concerns, or abilities. Related to ancient Olympia or Mount Olympus.

*Many thought Betsy's getting to medical school an **Olympian** feat, but her friends knew she would do it easily.*

O

omnipotent (ahm-NIH-puh-tent), adjective
Possessing complete, universal, unlimited power and authority. All-powerful; often used in reference to a deity.

*The framers of the United States Constitution sought to avoid making any branch of government **omnipotent**, so they created a system of checks and balances between the executive, legislative, and judicial branches.*

omnivore (AHM-nih-vore), noun
An animal that feeds on any or many different foods, including plants and animals. Someone who has wide interests, who will read, study, absorb, or devour anything available. From the Latin for "eating everything." A related word is *voracious,* meaning desiring or consuming food in great quantities, or eager about a particular activity.

*Most humans are by nature **omnivores**, but some choose to be herbivorous vegetarians instead.*

onerous (AH-nuh-rus), adjective
Burdensome; a lot of trouble. Describes a situation or agreement in which the cons could easily outweigh the pros. Something with heavy obligation.

*Although she loved her dog, Elizabeth thought that cleaning up the back yard after him was an **onerous** task.*

online (ohn-LYNE), adjective
Accessible over the Internet. Can describe resources, such as bank accounts, or activities, such as participation in chat rooms or games. Attached to or available through a central computer or computer network. Used to describe an electronic device or sensor that is connected directly to something being measured.

***Online** applications for admissions to college are becoming more prevalent than those completed on paper.*

onomatopoeia (on-uh-mot-uh-PEE-uh), noun
The naming of a thing by creating a vocal imitation of its sound. Examples are *hiss, buzz, whack,* and *splat.* One of the most fun words to know, use, and spell. How long is the list of onomatopoeic words you know?

*Comic books, which are filled with **onomatopoeia**, are thought to be the origin of many words of this kind.*

onslaught (ON-slot), noun

A powerful attack that overwhelms someone or something. A large quantity of people or things that is difficult to deal with or process.

*The **onslaught** of online concert-ticket requests temporarily crashed the computerized ticket sale system.*

onus (OH-nus), noun

Duty or responsibility, or the blame for something. The burden of proof for something in a legal proceeding.

*The **onus** of completing this long-delayed project now falls to you.*

opaque (oh-PAKE), adjective

Impenetrable to light, so images cannot be seen through it. Dull and without luster. Obscure and unintelligible in meaning.

*People who live in glass houses should not throw stones, and they should also dress behind **opaque** curtains.*

operatic (ah-puh-RA-tik), adjective

Belonging or related to the opera. Overly flamboyant or extravagant in behavior or appearance. Think "diva."

*Some of the students in Cathy's high school seemed rather **operatic** to their parents and teachers, and it wasn't a school for the performing arts.*

optics (AHP-ticks), noun

The study of light and electromagnetic reactions in the visible, infrared, and ultraviolet realms.

***Optics** has yielded inventions of common simplicity and good, like grocery store scanners, and some quite dangerous and powerful, like laser-guided missiles.*

optimal (OP-tih-mul), adjective

Most desirable, best, favored, or best possible. While everybody likes different kinds of ice cream, most of us consider it optimal to have plenty of it in the freezer.

***Optimal** game-time conditions would be sunny, but not hot, with little or no wind.*

optimize (AHP-tuh-mize), verb
To make something function as effectively as possible, or to use something at its best advantage. To find the best solution to a technical problem from a number of conflicting options.

*It took hours, but the mechanic eventually was able to **optimize** the car's gas consumption by regulating the carburetor.*

opulent (AHP-yoo-lent), adjective
Showing a lavish display of wealth or affluence; extravagant. Abundant in supply. Oprah is famous for her opulent gifts.

*The **opulent** lifestyles of musical performers and professional athletes are revealed in many television shows.*

oratory (ORE-uh-tor-ee), noun
The art of speaking in public with style, knowledge, and grace. Eloquence in public speaking. It can also mean a pompous, boring, or inappropriately long speech.

*Martin Luther King, Jr.'s **oratory** lives well into the present day.*

orientation (OH-ree-yun-TAY-shun), noun
Positioning of something, or the direction something is heading. Direction in which someone's interests or tendencies lie. Process of becoming accustomed to a new situation or surroundings, or a meeting to do so.

*It was the goal of almost everyone to be named as an advisor at the freshmen **orientation**, for it was an honor and a lot of fun.*

ornate (ore-NATE), adjective
Overwrought with elaborate or excessive decoration. Also describes language that is intended to impress with its flair or elaborate literary quality.

*Many parents who watch MTV Cribs think the homes of rock stars are overly **ornate**.*

ornithology (ore-nuh-THAH-luh-jee), noun
The branch of zoology that deals with the scientific study of birds.

*Few realize that Charles Darwin was well respected for his work in **ornithology**, in particular his detailed study of finches.*

orthography (ore-THAH-gruh-fee), noun

Writing according to the standard usage of a given language, using appropriate letters and symbols. The use of letters and symbols to represent the sounds of a language. The study of letters and spelling.

*The **orthography** of Spanish includes the letters rr and ñ, which have sounds different from those common in English.*

oscillate (AH-suh-late), verb

To swing between two points with a rhythmic motion. To keep changing your mind about which is a better of two positions.

*Robbie's mood swings **oscillated** so dramatically that his parents thought he might be manic depressive.*

Where'd That Word Come From?

Oscillate—This word for swinging back and forth derives from the custom Roman farmers had of hanging little masks representing Bacchus, the god of wine, from their vines. These little masks, called *oscilla,* would sway back and forth in the wind.

---

osmosis (oss-MOE-siss), noun

The movement of a substance through a semipermeable barrier. The gradual, often unconscious, absorption of knowledge or ideas through continual exposure rather than deliberate focused efforts.

*Too many high school students think **osmosis** an appropriate study technique; reading, writing, and rote memorization are still best.*

ossify (AH-suh-fye), verb

To change soft tissue, such as cartilage, into bone. To become rigid and set in a conventional pattern of beliefs, opinions, behaviors, or attitudes; also, to make others rigid and unwilling to change. Literally, "to change into a bone."

*As the years passed, Mrs. Wilson's dislike for freshmen seemed to **ossify**, until she was thought to be a burned-out teacher.*

ostensible (uh-STEN-suh-bul), adjective
Presented as being true or appearing to be true, but usually hiding a different motive or meaning.

The audience and critics thought the ***ostensible*** *purpose of the performers was to entertain, while the accountants thought it was to make money.*

ostentatious (oss-ten-TAY-shuss), adjective
Marked by a vulgar display of wealth, talents, possessions, or success designed to impress people; showy.

You shouldn't take the Rolls to the party; it will be seen as ***ostentatious.***

ostracize (OSS-truh-size), verb
To exclude or banish someone from a group, formally or informally.

It's harsh when teens ***ostracize*** *someone who was once a friend, yet shallow when they are welcomed back after a few days.*

Where'd That Word Come From?

Ostracize—It seems that a vote of banishment in ancient Athens had to be in writing. Because paper was scarce, the banishment ballot was written on pieces of tile called *ostrakon*, a name first applied to the shell of the oyster, which the tile resembled. It followed that the act of banishing someone from a group came to be called *ostrakismos*. Eventually, this evolved to "ostracize."

oxidize (OKS-uh-dyz), verb
To react or cause a chemical to react with oxygen. To combine with oxygen; make into an oxide.

When copper begins to ***oxidize,*** *it takes on what is called a patina, turning to a beautiful green color.*

ozone layer (OH-zone LAY-er), noun
The layer of the upper atmosphere above the earth's service where ozone collects and absorbs harmful ultraviolet radiation from the sun.

*Concerns over the depletion of the **ozone layer** grow annually, yet some still believe them to be unfounded.*

pacifist (PA-suh-fist), noun
Someone who refuses to perform military service or take part in war. A believer in the philosophy that international conflicts should be worked out through negotiation rather than war.

*Several of Zack's classmates had officially declared themselves **pacifists** during the Vietnam conflict in order to avoid the draft.*

pagan (PAY-gun), noun
A follower of a religion or sect that worships multiple gods. A heathen, or one who has little to no belief in religion, choosing instead to enjoy the pleasures of the flesh.

*The Crusades were fought by Christians against those they thought were **pagans**, yet today Islam is among the three major accepted religions.*

pageantry (PA-jun-tree), noun
Highly colorful, stately, or splendid display or ceremony, often with a historical or traditional theme. Most people enjoy the pageantry of a holiday pageant.

*The **pageantry** of graduation ceremonies is one of the reasons that they are so emotional for parents.*

paginate (PA-jih-nate), verb
To number pages of a book or document.

*Bill was amazed to see how easily the new word-processing software would automatically **paginate**.*

painstaking (PAYN-stay-king), adjective
Involving or showing great care and attention to detail.
The superstitious hockey player's preparation of his skates and stick before every game was painstaking.

palatable (puh-LA-tuh-bull), adjective
Having a good enough taste to be eaten or drunk. Acceptable to someone's sensibilities. Those with discriminating palates find only the finest food and drink palatable.
Very few of the actions of combatants in war would be considered palatable in peacetime.

palliative (PAL-ya-tev), adjective
Calming. Capable of soothing anxieties or other intense emotions. Alleviating pain and symptoms without eliminating the cause.
The little girl found her mother's singing of "Twinkle, Twinkle Little Star" palliative even during the times when she was most upset.

palmistry (PAHL-muh-stree), noun
Practice of examining the features of the palm to predict a person's destiny. At street fairs and carnivals, practitioners of palmistry are usually called fortune tellers.
While many doubt the authenticity of palmistry, many others regularly visit those who practice this art.

palpate (PAL-pate), verb
To examine the body with the hands and fingers, especially in a medical context. Not to be confused or misused as *palpitate*, defined next.
Medical students must learn to trust their fingers when they palpate patients, and not just depend on sophisticated lab tests for diagnoses.

palpitate (PAL-puh-tate), verb
To have the heart beat in an irregular or unusual way, because of a medical condition, exertion, fear, or anxiety.
Those who have been in life-and-death situations say that they heard their hearts palpitate and actually tasted fear.

paltry (PAWL-tree), adjective
Insignificant or unimportant. Low and contemptible. Often applied to ridiculously small amounts of money or lowly people.

*Some high school students think minimum wage is a **paltry** sum to be paid for an hour's work.*

panacea (PA-nuh-see-uh), noun
Supposed cure for all problems or diseases. Literally, a "cure all."

*Teens too often think that wealth is the **panacea** for all of their problems, but it is not.*

pandemic (pan-DEM-ik), adjective
Widespread. Something general, common, or all-encompassing, specifically an epidemic that affects people in many different regions or countries. The antonym of *endemic*, which is something occurring in a specific area or locale.

*During times of crisis, fear is **pandemic** and often the cause of more harm than good.*

pandemonium (pan-duh-MOA-nee-um), noun
Wild uproar, chaos, or tumult. A place or situation that is noisy, boisterous, and chaotic. The perfect description of almost any high school sleepover, at least those that are any fun.

*The celebration after the Giants won the Super Bowl could only be described as **pandemonium**.*

Where'd That Word Come From?

Pandemonium—English poet John Milton gave us this word for wild lawlessness, tumult, or chaos when he named the capital of hell "Pandaemonium" in his epic poem, *Paradise Lost*. He coined the word from the Greek for "all demons."

pander (PAN-der), verb
To indulge someone's weaknesses or questionable wishes or tastes. To appeal to the worst in someone. To serve as a pimp. Even if you speak with a Boston accent, it should not be confused with *panda,* that black-and-white bear indigenous to China.

*The director refused to **pander** to the wishes of some of his greedy advisors, and he left the film PG so that children could see it.*

Pandora's box (PAN-door-uhs bocks), noun
In Greek mythology, a box that Pandora unwittingly opened to release all kinds of evil and hardship into the world. In common usage, a powerful source of potential problems.

*Teens are warned that starting to use drugs is like opening **Pandora's box**, with consequences difficult to reverse.*

panoply (PA-nuh-plee), noun
An impressive display or array, such as a variety of riches. Ceremonial dress with all of the accessories; a full suit of armor and equipment used by a warrior. A protective covering.

*The **panoply** of materials at the Kennedy Library in Boston is quite impressive and one that both scholars and laypersons cherish.*

panorama (pa-noh-RAH-mah), noun
An unobstructed view that extends in all directions. An all-encompassing survey of a particular topic, site, or issue. A wide-view photograph.

*The Hendersons purchased the house on the hill because of the **panorama** that could be seen from the glass-enclosed den.*

papal (PAY-pull), adjective
Related to or pertaining to the pope or the papacy.

*The **papal** visit to New York City was a dream come true for millions of Catholics throughout the northeastern United States.*

paparazzo (pah-puh-RAHT-so), noun
A freelance photographer who follows famous people hoping to get a newsworthy photograph, story, or something shocking or scandalous. The plural is paparazzi.

Jim's family was a bit surprised that he chose to become a paparazzo, because his sister was a movie star who constantly sought to avoid photographers of this kind.

papier mâché (PAY-purr muh-SHAY), noun
Sheets of paper stiffened with glue or starch and molded into small objects including masks, bowls, and figures, as well as large objectives including floats.

The papier mâché piñata was filled with candy and was the hit of the birthday party.

paradigm (PARE-uh-dime), noun
A clear example that illustrates how something should work; an ideal instance, or a pattern worthy of study. In science, a generally accepted model of how ideas relate to one another, forming a framework with which research is conducted.

Kennedy's handling of the Cuban Missile Crisis is a paradigm for presidents who have to address challenges with courage, intelligence, and conviction.

paradox (PAR-uh-doks), noun
A statement, possibly true, that seems absurd or self-contradictory. A person or thing with contradictory qualities that are difficult to justify. Not to be confused with a "pair of ducks," unless you are the Marx Brothers.

Parents often face the paradox that punishment may be the kindest act of all.

paragon (PARE-uh-gone), noun
The very best example of something; a peerless model or pattern of perfection. Also, a perfect diamond or large pearl that is perfectly round.

Michael Jordan seemed a paragon among athletes, combining skill in basketball and competitive fire.

paralegal (pair-uh-LEE-gul), noun
Someone who assists and supports attorneys with their research and preparatory efforts. The Greek root *para-* means "beside," which means paralegals and lawyers work side by side.

*The role of **paralegal** is not given as much credit as it deserves, for attorneys are more prestigious.*

parameter (puh-RA-muh-tur), noun
Limit or boundary. Some physical property, such as size or color, that determines a thing's behavior. Not to be confused with *perimeter*, which means a boundary enclosing an area.

*In the military, there are very clear **parameters** for acceptable behavior and etiquette.*

paranormal (PAR-uh-NOR-mul), adjective
Beyond the realm of things that can be explained by scientific knowledge. Having to do with the occult, magic, or supernatural.

*It's hard for some to accept that **paranormal** phenomena do exist, and that all claims of poltergeists are not fake.*

parenthetical (pair-un-THEH-tuh-cul), noun
An explanation added to text as a commentary, usually set off by punctuation such as parentheses. A remark that departs from the sense of a passage.

*Sometimes **parenthetical** additions to writing are significant, and others are just afterthoughts.*

pariah (puh-RIE-uh), noun
Someone who is despised and avoided by others; a social outcast. In India, historically, a member of the lowest caste.

*It is sad that at one time people diagnosed with HIV were treated as **pariahs**.*

parlance (PAR-lunce), noun
A particular style of speech or writing, especially that used by persons in a specific context or profession. A way of speech, especially daily conversations, that is familiar to speakers who share common characteristics.

*The special **parlance** of doctors is one that laypersons find difficult to understand.*

parody (PAR-oh-dee), noun
A humorous or satirical take-off on something well known, such as a person or song. A literary or musical style or type. A poor attempt or imitation that appears ridiculous.

The Saturday Night Live *parody of the evening news has been a very popular segment of the show since its inception.*

parsimony (PAR-suh-moh-nee), noun
Great frugality, stinginess, or unwillingness to spend money. The state of being exceptionally frugal or thrifty. Parsimony is the ability to keep your pennies in your pocket; never parting with or parceling money.

Mr. Bench was, to all who knew him, the personification of parsimony, stingy and frugal to the extreme.

partiality (par-shee-A-luh-tee), noun
A liking for something or someone. An unfair preference for one person or thing over another.

High school students often accuse certain teachers of partiality, when, in truth these educators try to be impartial.

passé (pah-SAY), adjective
Out of date or no longer fashionable. No longer in prime condition.

It was once thought that bell-bottoms were passé, but fashion trends do return when least expected.

pastoral (PAS-tur-ul), adjective
Relating to rural or country living; having to do with keeping sheep or cattle. Relating to religious ministers or priests and their duties, or to the duties of a teacher. Pastoral scenes are often set in pastures.

The pastoral settings portrayed in the oil painting made them very popular among urban art buyers.

patent (PA-tunt), noun
Exclusive right to make or sell an invention. Official document setting out terms of a patent. Any official document that grants a right to someone. A government grant that gives someone title to public lands.

*Some who have **patents** are millionaires, while others are just proud that they invented something.*

pathological (pa-thuh-LAH-jih-kul), adjective
Uncontrolled or unreasonable. Related to disease or arising from diseases. Related to pathology.

*It seemed as if her lying was **pathological**, and it was impossible for her to tell the truth.*

patrilineage (pa-truh-LIH-nee-yuj), noun
Descent traced through the male line. A group of people who are related to each other on the father's side of the family.

*It is interesting to trace the **patrilineage** of one's family, seeing who was on your father's side.*

patrimony (PAT-rih-mo-nee), noun
An inheritance from a father or male ancestor. The things that one generation inherits from its ancestors. An estate or endowment belonging to the church.

*Much to the surprise of the children, who had never met their father, their **patrimony** came to more than a million dollars.*

patronage (PA-truh-nij), noun
The support, often financial, given by a patron, often to an artist or someone else struggling to express or invent something new. Support or kindness offered in a condescending way. The regular purchasing of goods from a business or store. Political power to grant privileges or appointments to positions.

*To encourage the **patronage** of young shoppers, Abercrombie was known to hire very attractive salespersons.*

P

patronize (PA-truh-nize), verb
To act as someone's patron. Also, to be haughty and condescending to people perceived as less important or intelligent. To be a regular customer at a business or store.

*Those who **patronize** others often don't have confidence in their own intellectual abilities, so they put others down.*

paucity (PAW-si-tee), noun
An inadequacy, shortage, or lack of something. Small number of something. If you have a lot of pets in your house, you have no paucity of paws.

*We were forced to head back down the mountain due to a **paucity** of supplies.*

peculiarity (pih-kyool-YAIR-uh-tee), noun
A characteristic or trait belonging distinctively to a particular person, place, or thing. The quality of being unusual or strange.

*George's need to whistle was thought the only **peculiarity** this well-respected man ever demonstrated.*

pecuniary (pih-KYOO-nee-air-ee), noun
Relating to or pertaining to money. Involving a financial penalty, such as a fine or fee. That which consists of or concerns money is pecuniary.

***Pecuniary** matters are rarely discussed by well-mannered families in public.*

Where'd That Word Come From?

Pecuniary—*Pecu* is Latin for "cattle." Cattle were once a common means of barter, so an estate's value was measured by its number of cattle. This led to the Latin word *pecunia*, for "money or property." *Pecunia* gave birth to numerous English words, such as *pecuniary*, "relating to, involving, or pertaining to money"; *impecunious*, "without money"; *peculate*, "to embezzle"; and *peculiar*, "pertaining to that which is one's own."

pedagogy (PEH-duh-GO-jee), noun
The science or profession of teaching.

*If students studied **pedagogy**, they would respect their teachers more and, frankly, be more likely to perceive teaching as a career option.*

pedantic (pih-DAN-tik), adjective
Lacking in imagination. Intellectually showy or overblown; making an ostentatious display of knowledge.

*Professor Anthony's **pedantic** manner was thought entertaining by some students and condescending by others.*

pedestrian (puh-DES-tree-uhn), adjective
Something ordinary, unimaginative, or uninspired. Pedestrian people are not necessarily pedestrians.

*The worst comment someone can make about an author's work is that it is **pedestrian**.*

peerless (PEER-luss), adjective
Incomparable, matchless, without equal; literally "without a peer."

*For old-timers, Babe Ruth was the Sultan of Swat, but for younger fans Barry Bonds is **peerless** in his ability to hit home runs.*

peevish (PEA-vish), adjective
Bad-tempered, irritable, or tending to complain; irritated by a peeve, or annoyance.

*Some parents think that all teenagers are **peevish** before 9 A.M. on weekdays and twelve noon on weekends.*

pejorative (pih-JORE-uh-tiv), adjective
Critical or disapproving; disparaging. A word or phrase that defames.

*It is sometimes difficult to distinguish between a sarcastic and a **pejorative** remark, but both can hurt one's feelings.*

penitence (PEH-nuh-tents), noun
Regret or sorrow for having committed sins, misdeeds, or wrongdoing.

*The time he spent working with youth groups reflected his **penitence** for the indiscretions of his youth.*

penultimate (pih-NUL-tuh-mut), adjective
Second to last. Not to be confused with *ultimate*, meaning very last.

*The **penultimate** player chosen in the National Football League draft is truly most anonymous, for ironically the last one picked becomes "Mr. Irrelevant," and the subject of much attention.*

perceptive (PURR-sep-tuhv), adjective
Quick to understand or discern things; showing an understanding of a person or situation. Related to perception or the capability of perceiving.

*As the older sister of three siblings, Stephanie was very **perceptive** of the needs of younger children, and she made a great babysitter.*

percussive (PURR-cuss-sihv), adjective
Having the effect of an impact or blow. An instrument that requires beating to make music; a drum, cymbal, or triangle. A long drum solo has a percussive effect upon the eardrums and on the brain as well.

*The **percussive** power of Justin's cross-check on the opposing player could actually be heard in the stands.*

perennial (puh-REN-ee-ul), adjective
Constant, enduring from season to season. Describes certain plants that grow and bloom from one year to the next. Also commonly used to describe hopes for things that are seemingly impossible.

*The state's **perennial** budget delays were expected, but not acceptable to those who depended on funds to provide services.*

perfectionist (PURR-fec-shuh-nist), noun
Someone who is unaccepting of any fault, especially in his or her own actions.

*Julie thought her teacher was a **perfectionist**, so she worked even harder on her essay.*

perfunctory (purr-FUNK-tuh-ree), adjective
Done as a matter of fact, routinely, without thought, attention, or genuine feeling. Not interested or enthusiastic.

*Responding to what he thought undeserving nagging by his mom, Hunter completed his homework in a **perfunctory** manner.*

periodic table (peer-ee-AH-dick TAY-bull), noun
The table that shows all known elements arranged according to their atomic numbers.
*Many chemistry students are asked to memorize the **periodic table.***

peripatetic (pair-ih-puh-TET-ik), adjective
Traveling from place to place, especially working in different locales and traveling between; wandering from one place to another.
*The **peripatetic** lifestyle of professional athletes can have a negative effect on their family and loved ones.*

peripheral (purr-IF-uh-ruhl), adjective
Concerning the edge or outside parts, as in a place or object. Being of minor or incidental importance.
*Mrs. Williams grew frustrated with the **peripheral** conversations that went on as she tried to lecture to her class.*

permafrost (PURR-muh-frost), noun
Underlying soil or rock that is permanently frozen, found mainly in polar regions.
*Digging a foundation during winter months in New Hampshire was like trying to hack through **permafrost.***

pernicious (purr-NIH-shus), adjective
Causing great harm, destruction, injury, or death. Wicked, meaning to cause harm. Fatal or likely to cause death.
*Though the initial symptoms were relatively mild, it truly was a **pernicious** and unstoppable disease.*

perpetuate (purr-PEH-choo-ate), verb
To make everlasting; to prolong memory of a thing or person.
*JFK's memory is **perpetuated** by the perpetual flame at his grave, which inspires both grief and hope in visitors.*

P

perquisite (PER-kwih-zit), noun
A bonus that comes on top of the normal benefits of a job, as in a tip. Something considered to be an exclusive right or a consequence of holding a certain title, position, or job.

*One of the **perquisites** of working for a baseball team is being able to get free tickets whenever you want.*

persecute (PURR-suh-kyoot), verb
To systematically subject a particular person, race, or group to cruel or unfair treatment. To make someone the victim of continual pestering or harassment. Not to be confused with *prosecute,* which means to have someone tried in a court of law for civil or criminal offenses.

*Prosecutors may want to, but they are never allowed to **persecute** criminals.*

perspicacious (per-spih-KAY-shuss), adjective
Penetratingly discerning, perceptive, or astute; able to understand easily or discern.

*While quite **perspicacious**, Lauren still made too many grammatical errors for her essay to earn an A.*

pert (PURT), adjective
Bold and lively in a pleasant and amusing way. Jaunty and stylish in design. Small, well-shaped, and pretty.

***Pert** was the only way to describe members of the women's gymnastics team.*

perturb (purr-TURB), verb
To disturb, trouble, or worry someone. To create a state of confusion or disorder.

*The baby's constant crying **perturbed** the neighbors, but the parents hoped they would understand.*

perusal (puh-ROOZ-uhl), noun

This word has two contradictory meanings. It can mean a detailed examination, as of a book or list of facts. It can also mean a casual, leisurely examination, as of items on the sale rack at your favorite department store. Look at the context to determine which meaning is appropriate.

*The editor's quick **perusal** of the manuscript led him to exclaim, "This is going to be a bestseller!"*

pervade (purr-VAYD), verb

To spread throughout or be present throughout; infiltrate, penetrate, or circulate widely. A cat's purr can pervade a quiet room with a sense of peace.

*When the crowd saw the paramedics quickly come to the aid of the injured player, anxiety and fear **pervaded** the arena.*

pessimism (PEH-suh-mih-zum), noun

The tendency to see only the negative or worst aspects of a situation or circumstance. The expectation that only bad or unpleasant things will happen.

***Pessimism** about Heidi's potential to pass permeated the family after they reviewed her second semester grades.*

pestiferous (pes-TIF-uh-rus), adjective

Troublesome or annoying; breeding or spreading evil, corruption, or infectious disease.

*Mosquitoes are the most **pestiferous** of insects, in all definitions of the word.*

petroglyph (PEH-troh-glif), noun

A prehistoric drawing done on rock. Literally means "rock drawing."

*The archeologists were ecstatic to find a **petroglyph** with animal figures.*

petulant (PEH-choo-lunt), adjective

Ill-tempered, sulky; impatiently peevish. Showing annoyance or irritation with minor problems.

*Children are often described as **petulant**, but it's more likely that adults exhibit these traits and behaviors.*

phenom (FEE-nohm), noun
An outstanding or unusual person or thing; someone or something phenomenal, remarkable, or impressively good or great. Not to be confused with *phantom*, which is something insubstantial and unreal.

Tiger Woods was recognized as a golf phenom when he was very young.

philanthropic (fih-lun-THRAH-pick), noun
Showing kindness, charitable concern, and generosity toward others; demonstrating benevolence toward mankind. Devoted to helping through charitable giving, bestowing wealth on public institutions or those in need.

The philanthropic efforts of alumni donors sometimes go unrecognized, but it is never unappreciated.

phobic (FOH-bik), adjective
Showing or having an intense fear and dislike of something, often to an irrational degree. Affected with or arising out of a phobia.

When he closed his eyes and tensed his body as the elevator reached the highest floor, his phobic nature became apparent.

phonetic (fuh-NEH-tik), adjective
Belonging to or associated with sounds of human speech. Representing sounds of human speech in writing, often with special symbols or special spelling.

Phonetic spellings are included in each entry in this book, so readers will know how to pronounce the words as they learn them.

photosynthesis (FOH-toh-SIN-thuh-sys), noun
The process green plants and other organisms use to convert light into an energy source. Happily for most other life forms, the byproduct of photosynthesis is oxygen, which means plants are responsible for the air we breathe.

When studying high school biology, we learned of the amazing biochemical process that is photosynthesis.

physiognomy (fih-zee-OG-nuh-mee), noun

The features of someone's face, especially when used as indicators of character or temperament. The use of facial features to judge someone's emotional state, inclination, or character. The character or outward appearance of something.

The physiognomy of television anchorwomen seem strangely similar, as if it were a job prerequisite for them to all look alike.

piazza (pee-AH-zah), noun

A large open square, this Italian word describes a common feature of most Italian cities, where churches and cafes can often be found. A covered passage with arches on one or both sides, usually attached to a building. A veranda or porch attached to a house. Not to be misused or confused with *pizza*, which also has Italian origins.

*The Billings family was inspired by a recent trip to Italy, so they built a **piazza** on the side of their home.*

picayune (pih-KEYE-yoon), adjective

Of very little importance. Trivial, not worth much. The famous New Orleans newspaper is called the *Times-Picayune*—perhaps a reflection of how party people in that fun-loving city feel about serious events of the day? Or, as you will soon learn, was that the price of the paper?

*The bride felt her soon to be mother-in-law's requests for the wedding were **picayune** and not worthy of consideration.*

Where'd That Word Come From?

Picayune—In early eighteenth-century Louisiana, a French copper coin and the Spanish half-real coin were called picayunes. *Picayune* itself most likely derives from the Spanish *pequeña*, "little," and the coin of little size and value influenced the term *picayune* coming to mean anything small, insignificant, and of little importance.

pictograph (PIK-toh-graff), noun

A graphic symbol or picture representing a word or idea. A chart or diagram that uses symbols or pictures to represent values. Petroglyphs are drawn in pictograms.

*Thank goodness the **pictograph** for the women's bathroom is universally understood.*

piercing (PEER-sing), adjective

A sharp, unpleasantly intense quality, often describing sounds that make you want to cover your ears. Also refers to powers of perceptions that are unusually acute.

*The scream Susie's mother made when she saw her navel piercing was indeed **piercing**.*

piety (PIE-uh-tee), noun

Strong respectful belief in a deity or deities and strict observance of religious principles. Devotion. Religious reverence; an inclination to worship God.

*The **piety** of the Monroe family was respected by all in the community, and appreciated when crises of faith arose.*

pilfer (PIL-fur), verb

To steal small items of little value, especially on a habitual basis.

*Even those teens who **pilfer** candy from the corner store should be prosecuted to learn right from wrong.*

PIN (PIHN), acronym

Acronym for "personal identification number," a secret code that gives an individual access to things like bank or computer accounts and other Web-based systems. People often refer to their "PIN number," which is rather redundant, if you think about it.

*Too many make their **PINs** easy to guess, so they are not safe from identity theft.*

pinnacle (PIN-uh-kul), noun

The highest or topmost point, as in a mountain or roller coaster. A natural peak. A pointed ornament on top of a buttress or parapet of a castle.

*Robert reached the **pinnacle** of his athletic career when he was named All-American after his senior season.*

pique (PEEK), verb

To cause a bad mood, anger, or resentment. To inspire intense interest, curiosity, or excitement. To pride yourself on something, especially in personal attributes or abilities.

*Marcia was **piqued** at not having been invited to the party.*

pithy (PIH-thee), adjective

Brief yet forceful and to the point, often with a touch of wit.

*The **pithy** speech of the captain served to inspire the entire team to victory.*

pittance (PIT-tense), noun

Very small amount of something, especially money, allowance, or salary.

*The workers were considering a strike for they believed they were being paid a **pittance**, much less than they deserved.*

pixel (PIK-sul), noun

An individual tiny dot of light or color. Together, a number of pixels form the images on a computer, television screen, digital camera, or printed image. Not to be confused with *pixie,* a tiny supernatural creature known for its nasty tricks.

*It's simple. The more **pixels**, the better quality the picture.*

placate (PLAY-kate), verb

To make someone less angry, upset, or hostile, usually by saying or doing something to please. To appease someone, or act in a way to avoid another's anger.

*It seemed to be our mom's job to **placate** the rest of the family whenever we were upset.*

plagiarism (PLAY-juh-rih-zum), noun
The act of presenting someone else's work or idea as your own. Something copied or someone else's idea presented as your own. Something no high school student would ever do—and that means you!

Plagiarism is the most egregious of all academic offenses.

plaintiff (PLANE-tuff), noun
Someone who brings suit in a civil court. Not to be misused or confused with *plaintive*, which means expressing sadness or sounding sad. However, a plaintiff will probably appear plaintive if she loses her case.

The plaintiff in the case seemed as motivated by the potential financial award as she was by the determination of right or wrong.

platitude (PLA-tih-tood), noun
A trite, commonplace, or useless statement made as though it was significant. You've heard them during speeches of candidates in high school elections, but you just never knew what to call them.

Often the introductions read by award presenters are filled with platitudes, and they are not sincere or well delivered.

platonic (pluh-TON-ik), adjective
Friendly, as opposed to romantic or sexual. Usually describes relationships between people who might be expected to be attracted to each other. Perfect in form, but not found in reality. The good thing about many high school relationships.

While teenage girls often seem okay with platonic relationships, for some reason they are less acceptable to teenage boys.

plaudit (PLAW-dit), noun
An expression of praise, gratitude, or approval. Applause is a public form of plaudit, especially when delivered in an auditorium.

Something laudable, like graduating cum laude, is definitely worthy of applause and a plaudit.

plausible (PLAH-suh-bul), adjective
Appearing believable; likely to be true, at least in a superficial sense. Persuasive in speech or writing. Pleasing but deceptive.

*Justin's explanation for the auto accident seemed **plausible** to his parents, so he was not punished.*

plethora (PLE-thuh-ruh), noun
A very large amount or number, vast quantity, oversupply, especially an excessive amount.

*The **plethora** of students enrolled in drivers' education classes revealed how important these co-curricular offerings were.*

plutocracy (ploo-TAH-kruh-see), noun
Rule of society by the richest people; also, a society ruled by wealthiest members. The overall influence of the wealthy, who control or influence the government or society.

*Some argue that almost all societies are in some way a **plutocracy**, for the richest people do have a great deal of power.*

poignant (POYN-yunt), adjective
Causing a sharp sense of sadness, pity, or regret. Appealing to the emotions. Acutely painful or affecting.

*The film's final scene is meant to be **poignant**, but I found it cloying and overly sentimental.*

polemic (puh-LEH-mik), noun
A passionate, strongly worded, and often controversial argument for or against something or someone. Someone who engages in a dispute or argues strongly or passionately. The art of argument.

*Attorneys are said to be professionals in the art of the **polemic**, and sometimes we think passionate politicians are as well.*

politic (PAH-luh-tick), adjective
Possessing or displaying tact, shrewdness, or cunning. You can see the connection between this word, *politician*, and *politics*.

*When called **politic** by his opponent, Peter thought it a compliment, until he learned otherwise.*

polity (PAH-lih-tee), noun

A particular form of government; a system of government. The aspect of society oriented toward politics and government. A state, society, or institution thought of as a political entity.

*The **polity** created by those who crafted the U.S. Constitution proved a model that many other countries adapted.*

pollutant (puh-LOO-tuhnt), noun

Something that pollutes with the introduction of products that contaminate the air, soil, or water.

*Few realized disposable diapers would be identified as a **pollutant** because of their plastic composition and not their content.*

polyglot (PAH-lee-glot), noun

Able to read, write, and speak many languages. Written or communicated in many languages. Someone fluent in multiple languages. Poly, the pirate's polyglot parrot, cursed in Portuguese and four other languages.

*Jordan left for overseas study an enthusiastic student of languages, and she returned a **polyglot**, able to speak Spanish, English, and French.*

pontificate (pon-TIH-fuh-kate), verb

To speak about something in a knowing and self-important way, often without qualification. To make a decree with self-righteous pomposity. To officiate when celebrating Mass, or making a church decree

*While she was well respected as an English teacher, students tuned out when Ms. Horner **pontificated** on the virtues of art and dance.*

portend (pour-TEND), verb

To indicate that something, especially something unpleasant, is imminent, going to happen; to suggest or foretell. Not to be confused with *pretend*, which means to make believe or to make others believe something untrue is true.

*The anxiety in Hugh's voice **portended** for his parents what to expect of his behavior that day.*

posit (PAU-zit), verb
To present or stipulate something for consideration; an assumption, suggestion, or fact.

*The detective **posited** circumstances that would explain the forensics of the
crime scene.*

potable (POH-tuh-bull), adjective
Suitable for drinking, not containing harmful elements. While potable water
is portable, they are not the same words.

*The presence of **potable** water was the one factor that would determine whether
the castaways would survive.*

pragmatic (prag-MA-tik), adjective
Concerned with practical results, rather than theories and thoughts; practical, useful, or apt.

*When confronted by the consequences of the flood, politicians who were usually
prone to empty oratory became quite **pragmatic**.*

precarious (pruh-KARE-ee-us), adjective
Insecure; unstable. Uncertain and subject to misfortune or collapse.

*The inexperienced campers pitched their tent in a **precarious** position, too close
to the beach.*

precedent (PREH-sih-dent), noun
An example from the past that is either identical to a current situation or
similar enough to it to use as a guide. Not to be confused with *president*, a
person who may be well advised to consider past precedents in his actions.

*The principal was concerned with setting a **precedent**, rather than with being
fair to the students who wanted to abolish the dress code.*

precipitous (preh-SIH-pih-tus), adjective
Done too quickly, without enough thought. On the verge of a dangerous
course of action. Very high and steep.

*Being an entrepreneur is a lofty goal, yet it can be a **precipitous** position,
requiring many risky decisions and much stress.*

precocious (prih-KOH-shuss), adjective
More developed than usual or expected at a particular age. Advanced, especially with regard to mental ability, as in a child's display of adult social or mental ability.

*Rene was a **precocious** nine-year-old who had already performed at Carnegie Hall.*

preconceive (pree-con-SEEVE), verb
To form an opinion or idea before information or experience is available to make an educated or fair judgment. Prejudice is almost always preconceived.

*Teachers sometimes have **preconceived** notions that boys are better at mathematics than girls.*

precursor (pree-KUHR-sur), noun
Someone or something that comes before, often considered to lead to the development of another person or thing. Someone who held a particular position before someone else.

*It is amazing to think that the typewriter, the television, and the tape recorder were the **precursors** of the personal computer.*

prejudice (PREH-juh-dis), noun
A preformed opinion, usually an unfavorable one, based on insufficient knowledge, irrational feelings, or inaccurate stereotypes. Holding opinions that are formed beforehand on the basis of insufficient knowledge. An unfounded mistrust, dislike, hatred, or fear of a person or group, specifically one of a particular religion, ethnicity, nationality, or status. Prejudicial people prejudge others.

***Prejudice** is an acquired characteristic that can be eliminated through education.*

prelate (PREH-lut), noun
A high-ranking member of the clergy, including a bishop, abbot, or cardinal.

*The pope is the highest **prelate** of the Roman Catholic Church.*

preposition (pre-POH-sih-shun), noun

The part of speech that shows the relation of nouns to each other and to the other parts of a clause. Examples include: at, about, and above. Not to be confused with *proposition,* which is an idea, offer, or plan put forward for consideration, or a sexual invitation.

*A prepositional phrase begins with a **preposition** and ends with a noun or pronoun.*

prescience (PREH-shehns), noun

Knowledge of actions or events before they take place; foreknowledge.

*Parents hope to have enough **prescience** to protect their children from future harm.*

pretense (PREE-tence), noun

Behaving in a way that is not genuine, but meant to deceive others. A claim, especially one that has few facts to support it. To falsely act or claim to be surprised. Make-believe or imagined. An instance of pretending.

*Many of Shakespeare's plays are crafted around ironic **pretense,** when men played the parts of women who were pretending to be men.*

pristine (prih-STEEN), adjective

So clean as to look new, unspoiled, not altered by human encroachment. In an original state; uncorrupted by later influence.

*For many teenage boys the **pristine** look and smell of a new car is intoxicating.*

pro bono (pro BOH-noh), adjective

Done or undertaken for the public good without any payment or compensation, most often in reference to legal services.

*Jay received the greatest financial reward from his corporate legal clients, but he got the most personal satisfaction from his **pro bono** work.*

proclivity (pro-KLIH-vih-tee), noun

An inherent tendency to behave in a particular way; especially, an attraction to objectionable or immoral activity or behavior.

*Wendy's **proclivity** to nervous laughter was distracting during employment interviews.*

P

procrastination (pro-kras-tuh-NAY-shun), noun
The act of postponing or avoiding doing something, especially as a regular practice.

Nick's procrastination led to last-minute and futile attempts to complete assignments.

prodigy (PRAW-dih-gee), noun
Someone who shows an exceptional natural talent for something at an early age. Something very impressive or amazing; a wonder, or marvelous example.

Anyone who can play in a symphony as a violin soloist at the age of nine is definitely a remarkable musical prodigy.

profane (PROE-fane), adjective
Used to describe language or behavior that shows disrespect for God, any deity, or religion.

Profane language seems to be accepted in the locker rooms of high school athletes, when it should be controlled.

profligate (PRAH-flih-gut), adjective
Extremely extravagant, wasteful, or shamelessly immoral. Extravagantly or recklessly wasteful.

Many rock stars take on profligate lifestyles after making it big, but some settle down in time.

prognosticate (prog-NAH-stih-kate), verb
To predict or foretell the future. To be an indication of likely future events.

Those television experts who try to prognosticate elections are often wrong.

promulgate (PRAH-mul-gate), verb
To proclaim or declare something officially, especially to publicize formally that a law or decree is in effect. To put forward publicly or announce in an official capacity.

News of President Kennedy's assassination was quickly promulgated throughout the school, even though no one but the principal's secretary had a radio.

propinquity (pruh-PIN-kwih-tee), noun
Nearness in space, time, or relationship.

The propinquity of the two families, who were neighbors for over twenty years, led to some close friendships as well as a few disagreements.

proscribe (pro-SKRIBE), verb
The act of condemning or forbidding something. The condition of having been denounced or exiled. Not to be confused with *prescription,* which is a written order issued by a physician authorizing a pharmacist to supply a particular medication.

After World War II, officials proscribed Japan's establishment of a standing army, which led to peace for decades.

proselytize (PRAH-suh-luh-tize), verb
To try to convert someone to a religious faith or political doctrine. To attempt to convert to one's religious faith.

Many are suspicious that born-again Christians all seek to proselytize others.

protagonist (proh-TA-guh-nist), noun
The most important character in a novel, story, play, or literary work. The main participant in a contest or dispute. An important or influential supporter or advocate of a cause or issue.

Holden Caulfield, the protagonist of the famous coming-of-age novel, is a character that many teens can relate to.

protégé (PRO-tuh-zhay), noun
A young person who receives help, guidance, training, and support from someone older with more experience or influence. Someone protected, encouraged, or helped by another of superior status or rank.

Historically, it seems that each vice president was the protégé of the president, but that is not the case.

protocol (PRO-tuh-call), noun

Rules of correct behavior on official or ceremonial occasions; formal etiquette, as practiced in diplomatic circles. Formal agreement between states or nations, or preliminary draft of a treaty or agreement. In technical terms, the rules that govern how computers transmit and use information.

*Official **protocol** requires that the American flag never be hung lower than that of another nation.*

prototype (PROH-tuh-type), noun

The original model; experimental or trial version of a system or invention.

*The **prototype** of the first personal computer is now in a museum.*

proverb (PRAH-verb), noun

A short, well-known saying that expresses an obvious truth and often offers advice; an adage. A popular saying, story, or maxim.

*The tale of the tortoise and the hare is a **proverb** that teaches lessons about life as well as sport.*

prudent (PROO-dunt), adjective

Characteristic of good sense, care in managing practical matters, and a tendency to evaluate situations carefully so as to avoid risk. Careful management of resources.

*Purchasing automobile insurance is always a **prudent** act, and one required by the laws of most states.*

prurient (PROO-ree-yent), adjective

Having or intending to arouse an unwholesome interest in sexual matters. Lewd, focusing excessively on sex.

*The U.S. Supreme Court has reviewed cases to clarify obscenity issues and clarify whether a book is **prurient**.*

psychosomatic (sy-ko-suh-MAH-tik), adjective

Caused by mental factors, as in illness. Describes disorders with emotional or mental rather than evident physical causes.

*When doctors could not identify any physical causes for her illness, they began to look for **psychosomatic** origins.*

puerile (PYOO-rul), adjective

Silly in a childish way; juvenile. Immature; related to or characteristic of childhood. From the Latin for "boyish."

*While Jack and Elaine were clearly in love, many thought his **puerile** actions around her inappropriate for a thirty-year-old.*

pugnacious (pug-NAY-shuss), adjective

Inclined to fight or be aggressive. Prone to quarrels or fights; given to conflict or dispute.

*On occasion, the coaches thought Kathy's **pugnacious** attitude was detrimental to her play on the soccer field.*

purported (purr-POR-tid), adjective

Supposed or claimed to be true, but without evidence or proof. Represented as the real thing.

*The **purported** sister of Queen Elizabeth was the star of the cruise, though no one could prove her relationship to the royal.*

purveyance (purr-VAY-yunts), noun

The act of supplying something, especially food. The task of providing, collecting, or requisitioning supplies for a king, queen, or army.

*The **purveyance** of materials for the wedding cost more than had been allotted in the budget.*

quagmire (KWAG-mire), noun

An awkward, complicated, or dangerous situation from which it is difficult to escape; entanglement that offers no ready solution. Literally, a soft marshy area or boggy patch of ground that gives way when walked on. For some, descriptive of many teenage relationships: awkward, complicated, dangerous, and difficult to escape.

*While building a new home at first seemed a wonderful idea, the project quickly became a financial and logistical **quagmire**.*

quaint (KWAYNT), adjective

Charming in an old-fashioned way. Strange or unusual in a pleasing or interesting manner.

*The students always thought it **quaint** that the alumni returned for the homecoming game.*

qualitative (KWAL-ih-TAY-tuhv), adjective

Having to do with the quality or character of a thing, often as opposed to its size or quantity.

*Dr. Burton would often criticize the research of his students as being too **qualitative** and not numerically driven.*

qualm (KWALM), noun

An uneasy feeling about an action or event; misgiving, pang of conscience, or concern regarding right or wrong. A sudden pang of nausea or feeling of uncertainty or apprehension.

*Katy had no **qualms** about returning to graduate school to earn her Ph.D.*

quandary (KWON-dree), noun

A state of uncertainty or indecision as to what to do in a particular situation. The state of mind of most high school boys and girls when deciding what to wear to a date.

*Elizabeth was in a **quandary** about what courses to take in the first semester of her freshman year.*

quantitative (KWAN-tih-tate-uhv), adjective

Able to be communicated in terms of quantity. Based on the amount or number of something; capable of being measured in specific numerical terms.

*Accountants certainly need to keep an accurate **quantitative** measure of their clients' interests.*

quant jock (KWAHNT-johk), noun

A phrase for someone who enjoys quantitative analysis; that is, applying numerical and statistical measurements to problems. Literally one who "rides the numbers," or is a "numbers cruncher."

*The graduate students thought being termed a "**quant jock**" to be a compliment.*

quantum leap (KWAN-tuhm LEEP), noun
A sudden, dramatic, and significant change or advance in thought. Derived from the behavior of subatomic particles, which quantum physics has revealed are able to travel great distances in almost no time at all.

*Crick and Watson's **quantum leap** from scientific research to creative thought revealed that DNA was a double helix.*

quarantine (KWAR-uhn-teen), noun
Enforced isolation to those exposed to a contagious or infectious disease. The period of time during which people or animals are isolated.

*The Mitchells thought it odd that even their goldfish had to be placed in **quarantine** when they moved to Europe.*

quark (KWORK), noun
An elementary particle; the smallest known quantity of matter.

*It's amazing how something as small as a **quark** can generate so much enthusiasm and interest in physics researchers.*

quarrelsome (KWAH-rull-sohm), adjective
Having a tendency to argue with people; tending to pick fights or angry disputes with others.

*You are not the only person she has gotten into a fight with; she is **quarrelsome** with nearly everyone.*

quasar (KWAY-sar), noun
A compact, extremely distant, ancient object in space whose energy output is equal to or greater than that of an entire galaxy.

***Quasars** were once theoretical, then only observable as vague electrical impulses, but they are now observable as clear images through the Hubble Space Telescope.*

queasy (KWEE-zee), adjective
Feeling ill in the stomach, as if on the verge of vomiting; easily nauseated. Causing a feeling of uneasiness or nausea. Again, like most teenage boys and girls before a date, or high school students before a test.

*Driving a long distance on the bumpy road made almost everyone on the team bus feel **queasy**.*

quench (KWENSH), verb

To satisfy a thirst by drinking. To put out a fire or light. To subdue a feeling, especially enthusiasm or desire. To cool hot metal by plunging it into cold water or other liquid.

Diligent students sometimes state that reading and writing is the only way to **quench** *their thirst for knowledge.*

querulous (KWER-uh-luss), adjective

Inclined to complain or find fault. Whining or complaining. Describing someone who makes peevish complaints.

The **querulous** *two-year-old felt better and stopped whining after his nap.*

quicksilver (KWIK-sill-vuhr), adjective

Tending to change rapidly and unpredictably. Literally "mercurial," like Mercury, the god who is also called Quick Silver.

The **quicksilver** *emotional transformations of manic-depressive individuals frustrate family members and psychologists.*

quintessence (kwin-TEH-sunts), noun

The pure, essential form of a thing, in its most perfect form. Something that is the most typical example, as "the quintessence of greed." In ancient medieval philosophy, the fifth element after earth, air, fire, and water.

The announcer commented that those who competed in the triathlon were the **quintessence** *of speed, strength, and endurance.*

quisling (KWIZ-lehng), noun

A traitor, especially someone who collaborates with an occupying force. Quiz yourself twice on this one—it's a word that means nothing like what it sounds.

Once the village was liberated, many of the leading citizens were now regarded as **quislings.**

quiver (KWIH-vur), verb

To shake rapidly with small movements.

It was hard to tell whether it was the cold or her nerves that was causing Jennifer to **quiver** *so much.*

Where'd That Word Come From?
Quisling—This word for someone who is disloyal at best, and an actual traitor at worst, derives from a Norwegian politician named Vidkun Quisling, who collaborated with the occupying Nazis during World War II.

quixotic (kwik-SOT-ik), adjective
Tending to take a romanticized view of life; motivated by idealism to the neglect of the practical. Hopelessly and impractically idealistic. Derived from the name of literary character Don Quixote.
*Susan's **quixotic** search for "Mr. Right" inspired her to take many singles cruises, but all she got was seasick.*

raison d'être (RAY-sohn DETT), noun
Something that gives meaning or purpose to someone's life, or the justification for something's existence. From the French for "reason for being."
*After teaching her first special education class, she knew her **raison d'être**.*

rakish (RAY-kush), adjective
Stylish in a dashing or sporty way. Having a streamlined look that suggests rapid movement through the water.
*The juniors all looked very **rakish** in their white dinner jackets, formal trousers, and athletic footwear.*

ramification (ra-mih-fih-KAY-shun), noun
The unintended consequence of an action, often one that complicates a situation or makes it harder to achieve the intended results. The process of branching out; offshoot or outgrowth, as in either ideas or actual branches on a tree or plant.
*Too many teens fail to fully understand the **ramifications** of their actions.*

ramshackle (RAM-shakl) adjective

Poorly maintained or constructed and likely to fall down, fall apart, or collapse. Shacks are ramshackle structures, ready to blow down at the first hard wind.

*Tourists were shocked and saddened to see the **ramshackle** huts where the poorer residents of the island lived.*

Where'd That Word Come From?

Ramshackle—What language did English borrow this word from? Greek? Latin? Nope—try Icelandic. *Ramskakkr,* "very twisted," is the possible Icelandic source for this word, meaning "loosely made or held together, rickety, shaky." Other possible origins include *ranshacle,* "to wreck or destroy by plundering"— which would make something *ramshackled* "wrecked or destroyed by plundering."

rancor (RAN-core), noun

Bitter, deeply held, and long-lasting ill will or resentment.

***Rancor** between the North and the South did not end for decades after the Civil War.*

randy (RAN-dee), adjective

Having a strong desire for sex. Again, like most teenage boys.

*Adolescent boys are, by nature, **randy**, but they seem to get worse over the summer at the beach.*

rankle (RANG-kul), verb

To cause persistent feelings of anger, irritation, or festering resentment. To feel slighted or annoyed because of a perceived slight, oversight, or criticism.

*The criticism of parents does **rankle** children after a while, but sometimes it is important to listen to.*

rapport (ruh-PORE), noun

A positive bond or friendly relationship based on friendship, trust, and a sense of shared concerns. Also, an established pattern of communication.

*The substitute teacher developed a good **rapport** with the students to ensure his own survival.*

rapturous (RAP-chur-us), adjective

Expressing or causing great enthusiasm, happiness, ecstatic feeling, or pleasure.

*Those who have the opportunity to see the Grand Canyon are often **rapturous** at the mere memory.*

rarefied (RARE-uh-fied), adjective

Seeming distinct or remote from ordinary reality and common people; lofty or exalted. Showing very high quality, character, or style: refined. In a scientific sense, having a low density, especially owing to a low oxygen content.

*When visiting the Oval Office, one is truly in a **rarified** environment.*

raucous (RAW-cuss), adjective

Loud and hoarse; unpleasant sounding, characterized by loud noise, shouting, and ribald laughter.

*The fraternity house was regularly the site of **raucous** behavior, as well as of visits from the campus police.*

ravenous (RA-vuh-nuss), adjective

Extremely hungry or greedy for something; predatory. Intensely eager to be satisfied, to gratify desires.

***Ravenous** as they were, the team could hardly wait through the introductory banquet speeches before starting their meal.*

ravishing (RA-vih-shing), adjective

Extremely beautiful, delightful, and pleasing to the eye.

*As you would expect, the bride was **ravishing** as she walked down the chapel aisle.*

R

recalcitrant (rih-KAL-sih-trunt), adjective
Stubbornly resistant to the control or authority of others. Difficult to deal with, work with, or supervise.

The high school principal's office was like a second home for some recalcitrant students.

recapitulate (re-kuh-PIH-choo-late), verb
To summarize in concise form; to briefly retell the essential points of a story. In terms of biology, describes what a fetus does as it repeats the stages of the evolution of the species during its development.

Great public speakers are known for their abilities to recapitulate and gesticulate.

reciprocate (re-SIH-pro-kate), verb
To give or act in turn following the lead of another. To give or do in return for something else. To reproduce the courtesy, gift, or example of another.

It was difficult to determine how best to reciprocate for all of the concern, caring, and help received after the twins were born.

reclamation (reh-cluh-MAY-shun), noun
The conversion of unusable land into land suitable for farming or other uses. The extraction of useful substances from refuse. The claiming back of something once taken or given away.

The reclamation of the inner city was deemed miraculous by those who lived there.

reclusive (rih-KLOO-siv), adjective
Withdrawn from the rest of the world; solitary and hermitlike. Shut off from the influences of the world or others.

After her husband died, Mrs. Hilton lived a reclusive life, rarely coming out of her house or speaking to anyone.

recompense (REH-kum-pents), verb
To pay someone for work or services. To give compensation for suffering, loss, or injury.

To recompense Mrs. Williams for all her suffering would be impossible.

reconnoiter (reh-kuh-NOY-ter), verb

To explore an area in order to gather information, especially about the position and strength of the enemy. To engage in reconnaissance. From the French, meaning "to explore."

The overly zealous coach, who was prone to military metaphors, said he would "reconnoiter" rather than scout the opposing team.

recoup (ree-COOP), verb

To regain something lost; to make up for something lost. To make up for something that has been lost.

Habitual gamblers think they will recoup their losses if they just continue their risky behaviors.

recrimination (ree-crih-muh-NAY-shun), noun

An accusation made by someone who has been accused of a crime, usually against the original accuser. Recrimination is often a very effective form of retaliation.

The press was shocked when the recrimination of one of his aides involved the president in the Watergate cover-up.

rectify (REK-tuh-fie), verb

To make something right; to correct an error. Technically, to purify a substance through distillation.

As people get older, they are often inspired to rectify past mistakes, particularly those associated with family and friends.

recuse (ree-KYOOZ), verb

To disqualify someone from judging or participating in something because of bias or personal interest. To withdraw oneself from judging or participating in something for personal reasons.

Seeking a balanced jury, the defense attorney recused many potential jurors until he approved of them all.

R

redundancy (rih-DUN-dunt-see), noun
A duplication, as in computer backup systems, created to reduce the risk of error or failure. Use of a word or phrase whose meaning is already conveyed elsewhere in a document or passage. Fulfilling the role of something already in place and functional; superfluous, no longer needed or wanted.

*Many functions of the spacecraft were designed as **redundancies**, that is, backup systems in case primary ones failed.*

referendum (REH-fuh-ren-dum), noun
A vote by the whole of an electorate on a specific question. Also, the questions placed before this group by a government or governing body.

*The results of the national **referendum** would not be binding, but it would tell leaders what the public desired.*

refuge (REF-yooj), noun
A sheltered or protected place that is safe from harm or threat. Protection or safe shelter from something or someone.

*Many Cubans seek **refuge** in America and risk their lives to do so.*

refurbish (re-FUR-bish), verb
To renovate or repair. To restore to a state of attractive completion.

*Volunteers **refurbished** the abandoned apartments in record time.*

regress (ree-GRES), verb
To return or revert to an earlier, less advanced, and generally worse state. To move backwards. To cause someone to reenact an earlier emotional state or related behavior.

*After she worked hard to raise her grades, a sudden illness caused Mary to **regress** in her study habits.*

regurgitate (ree-GUR-jih-tate), verb
To bring undigested or partially digested food from stomach to mouth. To repeat or reproduce what has been heard, read, or taught in a purely mechanical way without evidence of thought or understanding. Teens may prefer to say "hurl," "spew," or "toss cookies."

*For some courses, all that is necessary to receive good grades is to memorize and then **regurgitate** facts, figures, or definitions.*

reiterate (ree-IH-tuh-rate), verb

To say or do something repeatedly, often in a boring way.

*The candidate **reiterated** her views at each campaign stop and in every interview.*

relinquish (ri-LIN-kwish), verb

To give up or surrender. To give something up or put it aside, emotionally or physically.

*When he took ill, Tim's father **relinquished** many of the more physical household chores.*

remedial (ruh-MEE-dyuhl), adjective

Acting as a remedy or solution to a problem. Designed to help those with learning difficulties, or to improve skills or knowledge. Intended to cure or relieve symptoms of someone who is ill or challenged.

*While some students are too embarrassed to track them down, **remedial** services available for those in need are often powerful and effective.*

reminisce (REH-muh-NISS), verb

To talk, write, or think about events remembered from the past.

*It seems odd to parents to hear teens **reminiscing** about their elementary school years.*

remittance (ree-MIH-tunce), noun

The sending of money to pay for a service or merchandise. Money sent as payment.

*Credit cards seem to some as magic money, until you have to send a **remittance** to their issuer every month.*

remunerate (rih-MYOO-nuh-rate), verb

To pay money for goods or services, or compensate someone for losses or inconvenience.

*After the accident, the insurance company **remunerated** her for damages within twenty-four hours, so Martha got her car fixed quickly.*

R

renaissance (REH-nuh-sans), noun
A rebirth or revival, as of something forgotten or that was once less known or popular. Capitalized, refers to the period of European history from the fourteenth through the sixteenth centuries, regarded as marking the end of the Middle Ages and the rebirth or beginning of major cultural and artistic changes.

*The university's **renaissance** pleased its alumni, who were happy to see it return to its former educational excellence.*

renege (rih-NIHG), verb
To go back on or break a promise, commitment, or agreement.

*Some adolescents feel that parents often **renege** on promises of rewards for specific behavior, so family trust is tested.*

renunciation (re-nun-see-AY-shun), noun
A denial or rejection of something, often for moral or religious reasons. An official declaration giving up a title, office, claim, or privilege.

*Tim's **renunciation** of alcohol and drugs had such great consequences that he made others wish to follow his example.*

repartee (reh-pur-TEE), noun
Conversation consisting of witty remarks, or a witty remark or reply. Also, skill in making witty conversation.

*It was amusing to watch the girls practice their **repartee**, hoping not to be embarrassed on their first dates.*

replete (rih-PLEET), adjective
Amply and completely supplied with something. Having eaten enough.

*Grandma's famous Sunday dinners were **replete** with every tasty dish one could imagine.*

reprehensible (reh-prih-HEN-sih-bul), adjective
Extremely unacceptable and deserving of censure. Abhorrent and morally inexcusable.

*While her behavior was generally considered **reprehensible**, a few felt that she should be given another chance.*

reprobate (REH-pruh-bate), noun
Disreputable, unprincipled, or immoral person. Someone whose soul is said to be damned.

*Being called a **reprobate** was shocking to Blake, who thought his behavior normal for a teenager.*

rescind (ri-SIND), verb
To remove or overrule the authority of something. To reverse a decision or act, making it null and void.

*The appellate judge **rescinded** the original ruling, freeing the accused from jail.*

resilient (rih-ZIL-yunt), adjective
Able to recover quickly from setbacks. Able to spring back into shape after being stretched, deformed, or bent.

*Jane proved most **resilient**, as she was able to play in the season's final lacrosse game a few days after her knee injury.*

resolute (reh-zuh-LOOT), adjective
Possessing determination; motivated by or displaying determination and purposefulness.

*Americans seemed even more **resolute** to fight terrorism after the horrendous events of September 11, 2001.*

resonate (REH-zuh-nate), verb
To echo; to make something else vibrate or produce a similar sound. To have an effect or impact beyond what is apparent. To produce a sympathetic response; "get on the same wavelength" with someone else.

*The crying of any infant **resonates** with those who are parents, as they are sensitive to these sounds and the feelings they inspire.*

respite (REH-spit), noun
Brief period of rest and recovery between periods of exertion or after something disagreeable; a temporary delay or stay of execution.

*The coach felt the girls had earned a **respite** from wind sprints because they were working so hard during practice.*

R

restitution (res-ti-TOO-shun), noun
The return of something to its rightful owner. Compensation for a loss, damage, or injury. Return of something to the condition it was before it was changed. Attempt to repair damage caused by a wrongful act.

A bill authorizing restitution to the citizens interned in the camps recently cleared Congress.

restive (RES-tive), adjective
Stubborn and unwilling to accept rules or control; impatient with delay. Having little patience; unwilling to tolerate annoyances.

The restive players gathered around the coach, eager to get the game underway.

reticent (REH-tuh-sunt), adjective
Unwilling to communicate very much, talk a great deal, or reveal all facts.

On the first day of high school even the most outgoing students seem a bit reticent.

retroactive (reh-troh-AK-tiv), adjective
Reaching back into the past; effective as of an earlier date, especially in terms of contracts or agreements. Relating to or applying to things that have happened in the past as well as the present.

The reimbursement eligibility for those who paid the higher parking fee was made retroactive as of September 1.

retrospective (reh-truh-SPEK-tuv), noun
Something based on memory of past events, containing examples of work from many periods of an artist's life, or applying to things past as well as present. From the Latin for "backward vision."

The Warhol retrospective at the museum was amazing and so large that you couldn't see all of the exhibit in one visit.

revile (rih-VILE), verb

To make a fierce or abusive verbal attack; to curse or abuse in harsh language. To use insulting or abusive language; to denounce using harsh language. Something you may have done, but didn't know what to call it. Not to be confused with *revelry*, which means lively enjoyment or celebration.

*For some time Nixon was **reviled** by his critics, but after time he was respected and honored by many.*

rhetorical (ruh-TOH-rih-kul), adjective

Asked with no expectation of response; often describes sarcastic questions, or those the questioner knows cannot be answered. Persuasive and skillful, as in argumentation.

*The dean's **rhetorical** skills were much needed as he explained the new alcohol policy to the entire student body.*

ribald (RIH-buld), adjective

Humorous in a rude and vulgar way. Amusingly coarse, lewd, and off-color; often used to describe a joke about sex.

*The football team became infamous for **ribald** behavior, and on occasion they were disciplined for it.*

roguish (ROH-gish), adjective

Mischievous, often in an unscrupulous or dishonest way. Like a rogue; known to have low morals and bad habits. Playful.

***Roguish** behavior is not to be appreciated or imitated, no matter the reputation of the rogue.*

ruminate (ROO-muh-nate), verb

To think carefully and at length about something; to ponder or review mentally, over and over in one's mind. The Latin roots of this word (literally, "chewing the cud") describes the action of cows, who sit for hours on end chewing the same grass over and over again.

*Once they were admitted, the guidance counselor wanted every student to **ruminate** on which college admissions offer to accept.*

sagacious (suh-GAY-shuss), adjective
Possessing excellent judgment and powers of discernment; that is, able to make wise decisions. Keen and farsighted, in terms of perception. Call a teacher sagacious, and you'll be very pleased to see how they react.

*Professor Blake's **sagacious** reputation made him one of the university's most popular lecturers and advisors.*

salacious (suh-LAY-shuss), adjective
Lewd, off-color; intended to titillate or arouse sexually with explicit erotic content. Exhibiting explicit or crude sexual desire or describing deliberately provocative pictures or writing. Don't ever call a teacher salacious; you don't want to know how they will react.

*Some believe the more **salacious** the advertisements the higher the sales, especially to teenage boys.*

salience (SAY-lee-uns), noun
The quality of being important or striking. A particularly important or striking feature or relevant point of discussion.

*Teachers grade student essays on the **salience** of their thesis statements, supporting paragraphs, and conclusions.*

saline (SAY-leen), adjective
Salty; describes a solution of salt and distilled water, especially one having the same concentration of body fluids.

*Judy was so dehydrated that the doctor had to give her an intravenous **saline** solution.*

salutary (SAL-yoo-tare-ee), adjective
Promoting good health. Of value or benefit to someone; conducive to good health.

*The **salutary** effects of visiting a spa seem more psychological than physical.*

salutation (SAL-yoo-tay-shun), noun
A gesture or phrase used to greet, recognize, or welcome. The opening phrase of a letter or speech, addressing the recipient or audience.

*Brook was unsure whether to use the **salutation** "Dear" when writing to someone she had just met.*

salutatorian (suh-loo-tuh-TORE-ee-un), noun
The student graduating second highest in academic ranking. Something to strive for and be proud of.

*Being the **salutatorian**, rather than the valedictorian, is nothing to be ashamed of.*

sanctum (SANK-tuhm), noun
A sacred place inside a church, mosque, or temple. A quiet and private place free of interference or interruption.

*Many teens feel as if their rooms are **sanctums**, and they forbid anyone to enter without permission.*

sanguine (SAN-gwinn), adjective
Cheerfully optimistic; displaying a positive attitude. Also describes something blood-red in color, or flushed with a healthy rosy color.

*After the accident, Ken remained **sanguine**, speeding his recovery and inspiring the nurses and doctors who treated him.*

sardonic (sar-DON-ik), adjective
Disdainful; ironic in a mocking way. Extremely sarcastic and scornful.

*The more angry he became at his sister, the more **sardonic** Michael's comments sounded.*

satchel (SA-chul), noun
A small bag, often with a shoulder strap, used for carrying books and personal belongings.

*When the laptop computer became popular, everyone seemed to purchase and carry **satchels**.*

saturnine (SAT-ur-neen), adjective
Gloomy, moody, and morose. Describes things under the influence of the planet Saturn, which in astrology is known for its cold and surly nature.

*Oddly, after the death of his father, Harry became hopeful and optimistic rather than **saturnine**.*

savant (SUH-vont), noun

A wise or scholarly person, especially one with great knowledge in a very specialized field or area. Remember *Rainman*?

*In an irony of nature, some autistic persons who cannot communicate normally possess intellectual powers that can only be described as those of a **savant**.*

savoir faire (SAV-wah FAIR), noun

The ability to act appropriately and adroitly in any situation. An obvious sense of confidence and proficiency. From the French for "knowing how to do (it)."

*Amazing to his friends, Ron the quarterback demonstrated **savoir fare** during the debate competition.*

savory (SAY-voh-ree), adjective

Salty or sharp tasting, rather than sweet. Having an appetizing taste or smell. Describes foods that are not desserts, especially those made with meats.

*Mother's cooking was so **savory** that it could be smelled as we walked up the path to the front door.*

scapegoat (SKAPE-goat), noun

Someone who is made to take the blame for others. Someone who is unjustly blamed for causing upset or distress. Derives from an ancient Jewish practice of selecting a goat to accept the sins of a community.

*Students become livid when they think they are being made the **scapegoat** for the actions of others.*

scarlet letter (SKAR-lut LEH-tuhr), noun

Reference to the novel of the same name by Nathaniel Hawthorne, in which an adulterous woman was made to wear a scarlet "A" to mark her as a sinner. Now, a metaphorical reference to a sign that adultery or other sin has been committed.

*When word of her affair became public, it was as if she wore a **scarlet letter** on her clothing, for she was shunned by those who were once her friends.*

scathing (SKAY-thing), adjective
Severely critical and scornful, often referring to speech or writing about someone's conduct or performance.
The scathing review of the movie had no impact on its popularity or profitability.

scenario (sih-NAH-ree-yoh), noun
Outline of a play or dramatic plot, scene by scene. A screenplay. An imagined sequence of events that could become possible. Oh, a scene-by-scene story reveals a scenario.
Golfers have to think about all possible scenarios when they choose clubs for each shot.

schism (SKIH-zum), noun
Division of a group into mutually antagonistic and disagreeing factions. One faction formed after a disagreement. A division in a religion, or a breaking away from the religion.
Presidential elections recently have created schisms and anger among voters, rather than unified and motivated groups.

schmaltz (SHMALTS), noun
Exaggerated, histrionic speech or behavior meant to generate sympathy. From the Yiddish for melted chicken fat used for cooking and flavoring.
Planners often try to minimize the schmaltz when organizing fundraising events for fighting serious diseases.

schmooze (SHMOOZ), verb
To chat socially and agreeably. To talk persuasively to somebody, often to gain personal advantage. What high school students often do to get a better grade from a teacher.
Steve has been schmoozing his parents nonstop, a sure sign he wants something big.

scintilla (sin-TIH-luh), noun
A tiny amount of something. Also a spark, as in a small flicker of emotion.
The castaways preserved a scintilla of hope, along with a scintilla of potable water.

scintillate (SIN-tul-ate), verb

To give off or reflect light as sparks or sudden flashes. To dazzle in a lively, clever, or witty way. To excite, set off a sudden reaction among others.

*News about the new film has been hard to come by, but a few **scintillating** details have leaked out.*

scofflaw (SKAWF-lauw), noun

Someone who ignores, or scoffs at, the law.

*Eventually the **scofflaw** will pay for his actions, if not for his parking tickets.*

scrimshaw (SKRIM-shauw), noun

The teeth or bones of whales and walruses, engraved with detailed drawings, usually sea related.

*Collectors of **scrimshaw** understand how this art contributed to endangering whale populations, but they continue to cherish their prize possessions.*

scrip (SKRIP), noun

Paper currency or coupons issued for emergency use. A list, receipt, or short piece of writing. A doctor's prescription.

*During World War II, **scrip** was used to purchase gas and other commodities that were being rationed.*

semantics (suh-MAN-tiks), noun

The study of how language conveys meaning. An excessive focus on the way something is phrased, rather than what it says.

*The coach's urging to "play aggressive" rather than "hurt the opponents" was a matter of **semantics**, and its interpretation depended upon which team you wanted to win.*

semblance (SEM-blunts), noun

Outward appearance or show, usually not true. A representation, copy, or likeness.

*When the principal entered the classroom being taught by a substitute, there appeared to be no **semblance** of order.*

seminal (SEM-ih-nul), adjective
Highly original and influential, as in ideas that inspire later developments.
Relating to, containing, or carrying semen or seeds.

*For many, the Ten Commandments are the **seminal** expressions of laws, values, and societal norms.*

sentient (SEN-shunt), adjective
Capable of feeling and perceptions; the quality of being conscious or aware.
Capable of emotional response and of receiving impressions from the senses.

*Any **sentient** being should be able to notice the dreariness that comes with a cloudy day.*

sequester (si-KWES-ter), verb
To isolate, cut off from everyday life and outside influences. To take legal possession of someone's property until a debt is paid or dispute resolved. To seize or demand the property of an enemy.

*When the judge adjourned court for the day, he also **sequestered** the jury for the remainder of the trial.*

serendipitous (sare-un-DIH-pih-tuss), adjective
Accidental in a happy and fortuitous way. Often describes useful discoveries made by accident, or important insights encountered as fortunate coincidences.

*It was **serendipitous** that Phil won new golf clubs a week before the club championship.*

serene (suh-REEN), adjective
Clear and calm, without worry, disturbance, or stress. Bright without clouds.

*Visiting the lake house always made her feel **serene**, so she went there before her wedding.*

S

servitude (SIR-vuh-tood), noun
State of slavery, of being ruled or dominated. Work imposed as punishment.
    Being forced to paint the house in order to earn his allowance felt like servitude to Burt.

sesquicentennial (sess-kwa-sen-TEN-yuhl), noun
A 150th anniversary, celebration of a 150th anniversary, or a 150-year period.
    Historians reveal that the U.S. sesquicentennial celebration in 1926 was much more reserved than the bicentennial of 1976.

severance (SEV-runts), noun
The act of cutting one thing off or free from another. In business, compensation to an employee who is fired or laid off.
    Unsure of whether they would receive any severance, in the end they were happy to get three months' pay after the lay-off.

simile (SIH-muh-lee), noun
A figure of speech that draws a comparison between two things, using "like" or "as," as in "teeth as white as pearls."
    Robert Burns' famous poetic simile, "Oh, my love is like a red, red rose," is oft quoted and more often felt.

sine qua non (sie-nih kwah NON), noun
An essential condition, feature, or prerequisite. Latin for "without which not."
    Commitment is the sine qua non for academic success.

skullduggery (skul-DUG-guh-ree), noun
Practices carried out in a secretive way in order to trick people.
    The skullduggery of the Watergate burglars has become infamous, for it forced a President to resign.

sobriquet (soh-brih-KAY), noun
An unofficial name or nickname, especially a humorous one. Something almost every high school student has, although some just don't know what others call them behind their back.

*How embarrassing that she would call him "Pookie," a private **sobriquet**, in front of others.*

socialism (SOH-shuh-lih-zum), noun
A political theory that gives workers fair and equitable control over the goods and products they produce, as opposed to the free market principles and competition of capitalism.

*Historically, **socialism** has proven to work in theory only, with little success in real-world application.*

Socratic method (suh-CRA-tick METH-uhd), noun
A process of teaching and learning, in which the teacher asks questions that force the students to think and arrive at their own logical conclusions.

*Many of the best law professors use the **Socratic method** to teach students.*

solace (SOL-uss), verb
To comfort someone at a time of sadness, disappointment, or grief; to sympathize with and console.

*The family **solaced** each other with the knowledge she had fought her cancer bravely.*

soliloquy (suh-LIL-uh-kwee), noun
The act of talking to yourself, from the Latin for "speak alone." In theatre, a monologue that lets a character express inner emotions that would be difficult to communicate in dialogue.

*The **soliloquy** is a dramatic device made famous by Shakespeare.*

somnambulate (som-NAH-byoo-late), verb
To walk in your sleep.

*Kenny shocked his teammates when he **somnambulated** on their first road trip.*

soothsayer (SOOTH-say-ehr), noun
Someone who predicts the future through magic, intuition, or other imaginative means.

*Scientists are skeptical about anyone who claims to be a **soothsayer**, for they believe it impossible to foretell the future.*

sophomoric (sah-fuh-MOH-rick), adjective
Showing a lack of judgment characteristic of immaturity. Also, relating to sophomores.

*How strange and confusing it was to hear the principal call the junior class prank **sophomoric**.*

sordid (SORE-did), adjective
Demonstrating the worst aspects of human nature; immoral, tawdry, greedy. Undignified; dirty and depressing

*Biographies are often profitable publications, especially those containing **sordid** details about the lives of famous people.*

specious (SPEE-shuss), adjective
Attractive on the surface, but actually of no real interest or value; deceptive. Appearing to be true, but really false. Not to be confused with *species*, a biological terms for individual creatures that resemble one another and can breed.

*At first it was thought that archeologists found the remains of Jesus' brother James, but later all the evidence was proved **specious**.*

speculative (SPEH-kyoo-luh-tiv), adjective
Based on conjecture or incomplete information. Describes opinions or conclusions not based on facts. Risky, in terms of an investment that is potentially profitable.

*Even the most detailed statistical analyses of actuaries are only **speculative** in nature.*

spontaneity (spon-tuh-NAY-uh-tee), noun
Impulsive behavior that is not planned. Also, the source of such activity.

*The **spontaneity** of youth is looked back upon with great jealousy by elders.*

spurious (SPYUR-ee-us), adjective
False. Illegitimate, as in a child. True and believable but on the outside only. Forged.

*Eric's belief that his bad grades were because teachers did not like him was **spurious**, for in truth, he was very well liked.*

spurn (SPERN), verb
To reject someone's offers or advances with scorn and contempt.

*The fear of being **spurned** prohibits so many from revealing their true feelings.*

squalor (SKWAH-lur), noun
Shabbiness and dirtiness resulting from poverty or neglect. State of moral decay.

*The investigation found that because the three children lived in **squalor**, they would be better off in a foster home.*

stalwart (STAHL-wert), adjective
Dependable, loyal, strong, sturdy, and courageous.

*The **stalwart** support of his colleagues was what drove Dan to further achievements.*

stately (STAYT-lee), adjective
Impressive, dignified, and graceful in manner. Grand and imposing in appearance.

*First-time visitors to the White House are always impressed by its **stately** interior and impressive grounds.*

stereotype (STAY-ree-yo-type), noun
An oversimplified opinion, usually based on prejudice or poor judgment, held by a group of people, usually about people or ideas foreign to them.

*Bill Bradley, a Princeton graduate, professional basketball player, Rhodes Scholar, and U.S. senator lived a life counter to the **stereotype** of the dumb jock.*

stigma (STIG-muh), noun
A sign of shame or disgrace attached to something socially unacceptable.
Also an identifying mark.

*The **stigma** of having a child out of wedlock seemed to diminish in the late nineties.*

Where'd That Word Come From?

Stigma—From the Greek for "tattoo," this word for something that permanently stains someone's reputation comes from the ancient Greek practice of physically marking someone with a tattoo to distinguish him as belonging to a lower class.

stipulate (STIH-pyoo-late), verb
To specify a certain condition in an agreement or offer. To promise something formally or legally. In legal terms, to confess, admit, or agree to a fact, rather than require the opposition to prove the fact.

*The will does **stipulate** that you must wait until you are thirty years old to receive the money.*

subjugate (SUB-jih-gate), verb
To put someone, a group, or a nation under control. To cause to become subservient. To make another person perform your will.

*Throughout history, dictators' attempts to **subjugate** other countries have failed in the end.*

sublimate (SUB-lih-mate), verb
To bury and conceal the energy of an impulse or desire, usually one having to do with sex, in a pursuit considered more proper. To redirect an urge to a wholesome purpose.

*An artist who can **sublimate** his feelings might find them transformed into great works.*

sublime (suh-BLIME), adjective
Awe-inspiring beauty that seems heavenly. Of the highest moral or spiritual value; lofty, splendid, or complete.

*The climbers were rewarded at the top of the mountain by a **sublime** view of the valley.*

subservient (sub-SER-vee-unt), adjective
Eager to follow wishes or orders. Bending to the will of another; servile.

*In spite of how sexist it sounded, Ken thought that wives should be **subservient** to their husbands.*

subversive (sub-VER-suv), adjective
Intended to undermine a government or other institution, usually by secret actions performed from the inside; undermining.

*Antiwar protesters of the 1960s were thought by many to be **subversive** and by others to be patriots who personified the value of freedom of speech.*

succinct (suk-SINKT), adjective
Compact and clear, expressed without unnecessary words.

*Thomas's acceptance speech was **succinct,** lasting only one minute and composed of less than a hundred words.*

suffix (SUH-fiks), noun
A letter or group of letters added at the end of a word or part to form another word. An example: adding "-ly" to "quick" yields *quickly.*

*The **suffix** "ly" is the one commonly used for creating adverbs from adjectives.*

supercilious (soo-per-SIH-lee-uss), adjective
Contemptuous, arrogant. Disdainful and haughty; overbearingly proud. It's super silly for us to think someone so arrogant and haughty to be supercilious.

*Wealthy individuals sometimes behave in a **supercilious** way, as if money justifies overbearing behavior.*

Where'd That Word Come From?

Supercilious—Dr. Franz Joseph Gall, the founder of the "science" of phrenology, claimed that people with big foreheads and higher brows have more brains. This led to the expression *highbrow*, which described an intellectual. *Supercilious*, meaning "disdainful," is related to the brow, too. It derives from the Latin for "raised eyebrow," which comes from the image of someone lifting an eyebrow slightly in disdain. Think Jack Nicholson here (though most people probably don't think of him as a highbrow).

superficial (soo-per-FIH-shul), adjective

Having to do only with the surface; skin deep. Concerned with or stating only the obvious, with little significance or substance. Not thorough.

*The wound was **superficial**, requiring only cleaning and bandaging and no sutures.*

surreptitious (suh-rup-TISH-uss), adjective

Secret or sneaky, especially in terms of actions and acquisitions. Stealthy.

*Intelligence gathering is a **surreptitious** activity, accomplished covertly.*

sycophant (SIH-kuh-fant), noun

Someone who flatters a powerful person for personal gain; an ambitious flatterer who tries to improve his status by fawning over those in authority.

*Presidents and world leaders should not surround themselves with **sycophants**, for they need to hear critical and realistic views regarding critical issues.*

symbiosis (sim-bee-OSE-sis), noun

A mutually beneficial relationship among different species. A cooperative, mutually beneficial relationship between people, groups, or things.

*The two top students found that a **symbiosis** was much better than a competitive relationship, so they studied together.*

symmetrical (SIH-met-trih-kuhl), adjective
Balanced in proportion. Usually describes the even or balanced halves of a whole. Able to be divided equally in half.

*Whenever Mom redecorated, she first looked for **symmetrical** relationships between pieces of furniture, and then made me and Dad do the lifting.*

symposium (sim-POH-zee-uhm), noun
A gathering, for the purpose of discussing a particular subject and where learned people make presentations. A published collection of opinions or writing on a subject. Its plural is *symposia*.

*The **symposium** on how to teach high school students was very well attended by teachers and administrators.*

Where'd That Word Come From?

Sycophant—The old story, unproven but widely accepted, is that this word for an apple-polisher (basically, someone who sucks up to their superiors) originated in ancient Greece from the Greek *sukophantes* (*sukon*, "fig," and *phainen*, "to show"). This word referred to an informer on those who exported figs. At one time it was supposedly against the law to export figs from Athens, and *sukophantes*, later *sychophants*, often turned in violators of the law for their own selfish gain.

---

synchronicity (sin-kruh-NIH-suh-tee), noun
Coincidental events, especially thoughts or dreams, that seem related even though they are not obviously caused by each other. The great psychoanalyst Carl Jung used this term to describe an underlying connection of all parts of our lives, even those that we consider accidental.

*You have experienced **synchronicity** if you have ever been thinking of an old friend only to turn the corner and run right into her.*

synonym (SYN-uh-nim), noun

One or numerous expressions or words that have exactly or very nearly the same meaning. A word that means the same, or almost the same as another word; equivalent in meaning to another word.

If you are looking for a synonym, a thesaurus is a good place to start.

synopsis (sih-NOP-sis), noun

A condensed version of a text; an outline or summary of principal points.

Those small paperback books that contain a synopsis of the novels that high school students read are quite popular, and some are well written, but they should never take the place of actually reading the assigned work.

tableau (ta-BLOW), noun

A clear, descriptive representation of something; a picture. An artistic grouping of varied elements.

The prehistoric tableaus in New York's Museum of Natural History are so lifelike that they scare young children.

taboo (ta-BOO), adjective

Forbidden from use in ordinary context; reserved for special or sacred functions. Also, forbidden on the grounds of bad taste or immorality.

At one time having a child out of wedlock was considered taboo, but now it seems quite acceptable.

Where'd That Word Come From?

Taboo—The Friendly Islands (now Tonga) were visited by the English explorer Captain James Cook in 1777. It is in Cook's journals that we document the first use of *taboo* for something banned or prohibited. Cook had altered the spelling a little, from the Tongan *tabu*, which meant the same thing.

tabula rasa (TAB-you-lah RAW-zah), noun
Literally, a clean slate. In psychological terms, the mind before it takes on any impressions from society or experience. Also something that is pristine and new, without any preconceptions or existing features.

*Teaching kindergarten is so rewarding, for each child's mind is in many ways like a **tabula rasa**.*

tacit (TA-sit), adjective
Understood or implied without being stated; not spoken.

*Each juror's **tacit** assumption must be that the defendant is innocent until proven guilty.*

taciturn (TA-sih-turn), adjective
Quiet, of few words. Regularly uncommunicative or reserved in manner and speech. Someone who avoids conversation.

*Kenny was concerned that Emily's father's **taciturn** nature indicated that he disapproved of their dating.*

tactful (TAKT-ful), adjective
Able to say the proper things in order to keep good relationships with others. A tactful person is actually one who knows what not to say in order to avoid making others angry or upset.

*How **tactful** of her to decline his invitation by saying such nice things.*

tactile (TAK-tull), adjective
Able to be felt or perceived by the sense of touch. Also, related to the sense of touch.

*Velvet is pretty to look at, but it provides a mostly **tactile** pleasure.*

talisman (TAH-lus-mun), noun
An object believed to give magical powers to those who carry or wear it. Anything believed to have magical powers.

*Many indigenous people wear a **talisman** to ward off evil.*

tandem (TAN-dum), adjective
Two-seated, as in a bicycle. An arrangement of two or more items in which one is placed behind the other; single file. Also, acting in conjunction.

The team's warm-up featured a tandem lay-up drill that intimidated opponents and inspired the crowd.

tangential (tan-JENT-shul), adjective
Veering off from the main or current subject; departing from the plotted course. Peripheral. In math, relating to or involving a tangent.

Please stop; your tangential information is only serving to confuse our decision making.

tangible (TAN-juh-bull), adjective
Able to be perceived with any sense, but especially via the sense of touch. Able to be understood and evaluated with the mind. Things that are tactile are also tangible, though the reverse is not always true.

Sometimes tangible rewards of teaching, like salary, are not what truly matter, for the intangibles also pay off.

tantalizing (TAN-tuh-lie-zing), adjective
Attractive and tempting, often due to unavailability or unattainability. In Aesop's fable, the fox found the grapes tantalizing in part because he could not reach them.

College is a tantalizing goal for many students, but low SAT scores and poor grades make this dream impractical for some.

Where'd That Word Come From?

Tantalize—Tantalus, a son of Zeus in Greek mythology, divulged the secrets of the gods to the humans. He was sent to Hades and punished with eternal thirst and hunger. The pool of water he stood in dried up whenever he tried to drink from it, and the tree branches above his head pulled out of reach whenever he reached for their fruit. This punishment gives us the word *tantalize*.

T

Tao (DOW), noun

Literally, "the way." An Eastern philosophy founded by Lao-tzu and described in the *Tao Te Ching*. Basically, an expression of the ultimate reality, the universal energy that makes and maintains everything. The order and wisdom of life and harmony with the universe.

She was reading a book with a more philosophical look at relationships called The **Tao** *of Dating.*

tautology (tow-TAH-luh-gee), noun

A redundant repetition of meaning in a sentence or idea using different words. Unnecessary repetition—in different words—of an idea already stated.

*Stating that you know a foreigner from another nation is a **tautology**, because all foreigners are from other countries.*

taxonomy (tak-SAH-nuh-mee), noun

A logical system that describes the interrelationships of different things. In biology, the classification that assigns every organism a Latin name according to its genus and species, thus identifying its relation to other similar beings and its place in the system overall.

*Prior to creating a lesson plan, each teacher must develop a **taxonomy** of learning objectives.*

technocrat (tek-NUH-krat), noun

A bureaucrat with training in engineering, economics, or some form of technology. Someone who believes that technicians, or the people who know how things actually work, should be the ones involved in government.

*Stereotypically, **technocrats** think less about emotional issues and how decisions impact people.*

tectonic (tek-TAH-nik) adjective

Having to do with the geological structure of the earth, particularly the earth's crust. The study of *tectonics* investigates the way a planet's crust works, forming mountains and causing earthquakes.

Tectonic plates are geologic features that some believe will cause a major earthquake with an epicenter in California.

T

telekinesis (tel-uh-kuh-NEE-siss), noun
The supposed psychic power to move objects with the mind. From the Greek roots for "from a distance" and "movement."

*Some comic book characters are known for their powers of **telekinesis**.*

temblor (TEM-blor), noun
An earthquake. From the Spanish verb meaning "to quake." Not a *trembler*, as some think, but in the same vein as *tremor*, which is a shaking or vibration before or after an earthquake.

*Since the last earthquake all new construction was required to be built to withstand large **temblors**.*

temerity (tuh-MARE-uh-tee), noun
Reckless confidence that may be offensive. Brashness; reckless disregard of danger or unpleasant consequences. Fearlessness is not always a good thing.

*The **temerity** of being a teen often leads to reckless behavior and sadness for parents.*

temperance (TEM-puh-rense), noun
Self-restraint in the face of temptation; moderation. Abstinence from drinking alcohol. What every parent hopes their high school student practices.

*The new coaching staff demanded **temperance** of the football team during the season.*

tempest (TEM-pust), noun
A severe storm with high winds, rain, hail, or snow. A severe commotion or disturbance, especially with emotional upheaval. Turbulent, giving rise to many violent emotions or stormy actions.

*The **tempest** of Jim and Stephanie's argument was embarrassing to those who witnessed it.*

template (TEM-plut), noun
A master pattern from which other identical copies can be made; a pattern.

*I've heard the secret to woodworking is to make a detailed **template** of each part before it is cut or carved.*

temporal (TEM-puh-rul), adjective
Connected with life in the world, rather than spiritual life. Lasting only a short time. Related to or existing in time, as opposed to space.

*The **temporal** issues associated with manned spaceflight to Mars are as complicated as the mechanical.*

tenable (TEH-nuh-bull), adjective
Justified in a fair or rational way; defensible based on sufficient evidence. Able to be maintained, held, or defended against attack.

*Investors determined that further support of the company's owners was no longer **tenable**, so they approved a takeover.*

tenacity (tuh-NA-suh-tee), noun
The quality of being unyielding; stubborn. The ability or tendency to stick firmly to a decision or opinion, without doubt or potential to change. The strength with which something sticks, holds together, or clings, particularly to a surface.

*Marybeth's **tenacity** was evident when she played the entire second half with a broken arm.*

tenet (TEH-nut), noun
A set of established and fundamental beliefs, especially related to religion or politics; a principle. A fundamental belief held essential by a society, group, or organization. Not a *tenant*, who is someone who rents a property.

*The **tenet** that "All politics is local" is one that few candidates forget.*

tenuous (TEN-yoo-uss), adjective
Not based on anything substantial or significant; liable to break down easily when challenged. Thin, diluted, or insubstantial. Literally, means "slender (as a thread)." Not to be confused with *tenacious*, which has the opposite meaning of holding tight and sticking firmly.

*The couple's relationship seemed **tenuous** at best, but their families hoped they could reconcile and stay married.*

tenure (TEN-yur), noun

The holding of an official position, or the length of time that position is held.

Raises are based on performance rather than tenure, so some who have been here a while might not be compensated as well as newcomers.

terminus (TUR-mih-nus), noun

The end points of a fixed transportation route, such as the beginning and end of a railroad or bus line. A point where something stops or reaches its end.

When developers learned that Maplewood would become the terminus for the new rail system to New York City, they began buying up properties quickly.

terra cotta (TARE-uh KAH-tuh), noun

Pottery of a distinctive reddish-brown, usually unglazed at least in part. The earthenware clay used to make such pieces. The brownish-red color itself.

Native American pottery made of terra cotta has become very popular among collectors of late.

terra firma (TARE-uh FER-muh), noun

Solid ground; not water or air. From the Latin for "firm ground."

After the harrowing airline flight, the passengers were so grateful to be on terra firma that they kissed the ground.

tertiary (TUR-shee-are-ee), adjective

Third in order, place, importance, or succession. Third in a list, sequence, or progression.

Because the first two did not work, the tertiary option, using military action, was being discussed by leaders in private.

testament (TESS-tuh-mint), noun

Proof that something else exists or is true. A tribute. Also, a formal statement or speech outlining beliefs. The act of determining how property will be divided after death; a will.

The success of his son was a testament to his parenting skills and love.

testimonial (TESS-tuh-moh-nee-yul), noun
A favorable report supporting the existence of a thing's qualities and virtues.
A statement backing a claim or supporting facts. Something done or given
in honor or gratitude for someone.

*At the honors ceremony, Jane offered a **testimonial** to all the teachers who had
done so much to help her achieve all that she had.*

tête-à-tête (TET ah TET), noun
A private conversation between two people; a face-to-face meeting. French
for "head-to-head."

*Soon after the wedding, the mother of the bride and mother of the groom had
a lively and necessary **tête-à-tête** to address issues of the marriage.*

theism (THEE-ih-zum), noun
Belief in the divine, in the form of one or many gods. Usually, the belief that
one god created the world and is still evident in the works of creation. It is
important to note that theism is part of many different religions, not just
those that follow the Bible.

*As early civilizations progressed, **theism** became prominent and the worship-
ing of idols largely disappeared.*

theorem (THEE-uh-rum), noun
A proposition or formula in mathematics or logic that can be proved from a
set of basic assumptions. An idea that is accepted or proposed as true.

*The Pythagorean **theorem** is memorized by all students and is used as a foundation for many mathematical proofs.*

thesaurus (thuh-SOH-rus), noun
A book that lists words related to each other in meaning, usually presenting
synonyms and antonyms.

*Today, word-processing software usually includes a dictionary, a **thesaurus**,
and a spell checker.*

thespian (THESS-pee-un), noun
An actor, especially a person who performs onstage in a play.

*Thespian is an old-fashioned term for an actor, but it is one that some per-
formers prefer.*

think tank (THINK tahnk), noun
A group of experts that researches certain subjects, comes up with solutions to complex problems, and gives advice, most often to the government.

After graduation, many students of Political Science sought positions with **think tanks**, *so they could continue their research.*

Third World (THERD werld), noun
In general, developing nations with minor economies. The bigger capitalist industrialized nations are called the First World, and the industrialized communist nations were known as the Second World.

The debt of **Third World** *nations was so large it had to be excused, for if payment were demanded countries would be bankrupt.*

thoracic (thoh-RA-sick), adjective
Involving or located in the chest.

The family feared what the **thoracic** *surgeon had to say about the procedure.*

throng (THRONG), noun
A large crowd of persons or objects. Definitely not to be used or confused with *thong*, a very brief type of underwear or swimsuit bottom.

Let's wait here for fifteen minutes to avoid the **throng** *of people trying to get to their cars in the parking lot.*

thwart (THWORT), verb
To oppose, confuse, or defeat. To keep someone from achieving their goals or plans.

Steve's plan to surprise his parents was **thwarted** *when his little sister left their present out in the open.*

tirade (TIE-raid), noun
A long, overblown, angry speech, most often a criticism or denunciation; an extended outburst of harsh talk.

Sadly, Frank had come to fear his wife's **tirades** *so much that he avoided coming home.*

titillate (TIH-tuh-late), verb

To excite or stimulate someone in a pleasurable way.

*Stories about rock star romances seems always to **titillate**, no matter how old the listeners.*

tome (TOAM), noun

A thick or heavy book on a serious subject. A scholarly book on an academic subject.

*Aren't you lucky you're reading a short book on words, rather than a **tome** on the history of the English language?*

tort (TOART), noun

In legal terms, a wrongful act for which damages can be sought by an injured party. Not to be confused with *torte,* a rich cake of many layers sandwiched together with cream filling.

*Law students find classes on **torts** to be the most interesting and, ultimately, when they practice law, the most practical.*

totalitarian (toh-TA-luh-tare-yun), adjective

Centralized, in terms of official government power. Describes a form of government in which control is concentrated in the hands of one ruler or party, with no opposition permitted. Adolf Hitler and Joseph Stalin both led totalitarian regimes, even though they came from opposite ends of the political spectrum.

*The **totalitarian** state of the Soviet Union ultimately fell, decades after it was founded.*

traduce (tra-DOOCE), verb

To lie and create false impressions in order to make something or someone seem shameful or bad. It's easy to deduce when one does traduce, just by listening to the mean things being said.

*Angry over one thing or another, Page **traduced** her sister so frequently that her parents had to intervene.*

T

trajectory (truh-JEK-tuh-ree), noun
The path a projectile makes in space under the action of forces including thrust, wind, and gravity. The course a flying object takes after takeoff.
*The **trajectory** of all flights was being monitored and guided by the air traffic controllers.*

tranquil (TRAN-kwill), adjective
Calm, quiet. Free of disturbance or commotion. Unagitated, with no signs of anxiety or agitation.
*After years of looking for the best vacation location, the Burtons found their lake home to be the most **tranquil** place.*

transfiguration (tranz-FIG-yoor-ay-shun), noun
A dramatic change in appearance, especially one that glorifies or exalts someone.
*The popular make-over shows bring about physical and emotional **transfigurations** for their participants.*

transfix (tranz-FICKS), verb
To make someone temporarily unable to move; to hold motionless. To pierce someone or something through with a weapon or sharp object.
*The deer stood **transfixed**, paralyzed by the headlights of the car.*

transgress (tranz-GRESS), verb
To cross a line and do something wrong, often disobeying a command, guideline, moral code, or law. To go beyond a limit, usually in a bad way.
*David **transgressed** by crossing into Mr. Peterson's yard to play ball.*

transliterate (tranz-LIT-uh-rate), verb
Literally, "to write across." To write words from other languages in a familiar alphabet. Even if the meaning of the foreign word is unknown, through transliteration it can at least be properly pronounced.
*Thank goodness the prayer book was **transliterated**, for they did not know how to read the Hebrew alphabet.*

transpire (tranz-PIRE), verb
To give off water vapor, especially through the surfaces of plant leaves. To be exposed; to come to light and become known. To occur.

*As they recalled, the events of the accident seemed to **transpire** in slow motion.*

travail (truh-VALE), verb
To work hard, especially over a long period of time, at a physically demanding job. Sometimes used to describe the labor of childbirth.

*Harriet **travailed** all the way through her chemotherapy, which some say is as painful as the illness.*

treachery (TREH-chuh-ree), noun
An act of betrayal or deceit; treason. A severe violation of trust.

*Benedict Arnold's name has become synonymous with the words **treachery** and traitor.*

treatise (TREE-tiss), noun
A scholarly, formal written work that deals extensively with a given subject. A systematic essay or written argument on a particular subject. What you will be able to write once you incorporate these words into your vocabulary.

*Freud's **treatise** on psychoanalysis and causes of mental illness was controversial for its time.*

trepidation (tre-pih-DAY-shun), noun
Fear about the future or a particular future event. Involuntary trembling.

*A look of **trepidation** was visible on his mother's face when Justin went for his first driving lesson.*

triage (TREE-ahj), noun
The process of prioritizing sick or injured people for treatment, according to severity and condition.

*It was amazing to see how calmly **triage** was completed at the site of the train crash.*

tribunal (trie-BYOO-nul), noun
A defense, usually unofficial, of the rights of an individual. Also a court or other forum where justice is meted out. If you've ever wondered why so many newspapers are called the *Tribune*, the first definition of this word should be your answer.

*The military **tribunal** was formed to judge those suspected of terrorist activities.*

trite (TRYTE), adjective
Overused; lacking in interest or originality. Something you don't want someone to say about your writing or speech, so read and use this book!

*Oh, how **trite** every interview with a political candidate sounds.*

tropism (TROH-piz-uhm), noun
A natural inclination or propensity to react in a given way to a certain stimulus. Comedians hope that laughter is a tropism that characterizes their act.

*All of the plants in the room leaned toward the window as a result of their **tropism** toward light.*

tryst (TRIST), noun
A prearranged meeting, especially one made privately or secretly between lovers. Originally meant "to make an arrangement with."

*Both were nervous planning their **tryst**, for they feared their affair would somehow be revealed.*

tumult (tuh-MULT), noun
A violent, chaotic, or noisy commotion; an uproar. A psychological or emotional upheaval or agitation. Major mudslides cause tumult.

*The **tumult** of having twenty two-year-olds in the house for a birthday party was too much for Lisa's mother to handle.*

ubiquitous (yoo-BIK-wi-tuss), adjective
Seemingly present everywhere at once. So common as to appear to be all places.

*Some think the Mercedes has become a **ubiquitous** symbol of wealth, while others consider it one of conspicuous consumption.*

ultimatum (ul-tih-MAY-tum), noun

An expression that includes a demand along with the consequences, usually negative, of failing to meet the demand. A set of terms that cannot be compromised, without predetermined consequences occurring.

*Either pay the rent by midnight on the thirty-first, or be thrown out in the street: that was Simon's **ultimatum**.*

umbrage (UM-brij), noun

Resentment or annoyance arising from an offense; something or someone causing intense irritation.

*Principal Michaels took **umbrage** at the suggestion that he was only concerned with test scores, and not with students.*

uncharted (UHN-chart-uhd), adjective

Not surveyed or recorded on a map. Not previously encountered, experienced, or investigated. Often confused with *unchartered,* meaning not officially authorized or permitted by a governing body.

*Boldly but stupidly, the group decided to embark on **uncharted** waters in their small boat.*

unctuous (UNG-chwuhs), adjective

Slippery and greasy; oily. Smug and obsequious in an attempt to charm or convince. Describes a texture that is soft and smooth, like an oil or ointment. Containing or composed of oil or fat.

*Mud baths may not be healing, but they can be soothing, and they are most definitely **unctuous**.*

undaunted (un-DAHN-tud), adjective

Not put off or deterred by the prospect or even the likelihood of failure, loss, or defeat.

***Undaunted**, the underdog football team faced the state champions and almost won.*

U

underhanded (un-dur-HAN-dud), adjective

Secret and dishonest, with intention to deceive or cheat. Most underhanded people seek to get the upper hand any way they can.

His attempts to discredit his opponent with rumors and lies were definitely underhanded.

Where'd That Word Come From?

Underhanded—Card sharks are proficient at palming cards, holding extra cards under their hands. The word *underhanded,* "in a secret or stealthy manner," eventually came to refer to anyone who steals from or takes advantage of another in a sneaky and crafty way.

---

underling (UN-dur-ling), noun

A servant or subordinate, especially one regarded with contempt or as of little importance.

Robin was not Batman's underling; he was his crime-fighting partner.

underwrite (UN-dur-wryt), verb

To insure someone or something by accepting liability for losses. To guarantee the sale of an issue of securities at a predetermined price. To agree to provide funds or cover any losses.

The fledgling filmmakers asked parents and friends to underwrite their first feature film.

unflinching (un-FLIHN-ching), adjective

Strong and unhesitating, especially in the face of difficulty. Courageous.

Mary's unflinching dedication to her children was evidenced by her holding two jobs.

unilateral (yoo-nih-LA-tuh-rul), adjective
Undertaken independently, as in decisions made by only one of many political parties. One-sided. Also, responsibility born by or imposed upon one party or individual.

*The allies resolved that no member country would take any **unilateral** action that might threaten mutual security.*

unorthodox (un-OR-thuh-docks), adjective
Not following conventional or traditional beliefs or practices. Not practicing or conforming to or accepting traditional religious practices.

*Her teaching methods may be **unorthodox**, but they clearly get results, as all of her students passed the state exam.*

unpalatable (un-puh-LA-tuh-bull), adjective
Having an unpleasant taste or effect; disagreeable and undesirable. Not pleasant, acceptable, or agreeable.

*I am surprised that you didn't understand that the consequences for your bad behavior would be **unpalatable**.*

unrefined (un-ree-FIND), adjective
In a natural state; not processed, with all impurities still intact. Displaying poor social graces; unschooled in approved tastes and behaviors.

*Snobs at the country club shunned those they thought **unrefined**.*

unsavory (un-SAY-voh-ree), adjective
Tasteless, bland; unappetizing. Morally unacceptable or distasteful. Similar to *unseemly*, which means contrary to accepted standards of good taste or acceptable behavior, or occurring at an inconvenient time or place.

*How scared were you when we went into that twenty-four-hour diner full of **unsavory** characters?*

uproarious (up-ROAR-ee-yus), adjective
Defined by noisy confusion; loud and boisterous. Extremely funny and causing people to laugh aloud.

*I hear the new headliner at the comedy club has an **uproarious** routine.*

urbane (urr-BAYN), adjective
Sophisticated, refined, or courteous. Well versed in the social graces. Not to be confused with *urban*, which means related to a city. Some urban dwellers are urbane, though not all.

*Jordan could not stop talking about how **urbane** everyone was on her cruise to England.*

urban myth (UR-bun mith), noun
A bizarre story in wide circulation, presented as though the events actually happened. Characterized by the fact that the person telling the story never experienced the events herself but always knows a friend or aunt or other third party who can vouch for their truthfulness.

*One of the most often repeated **urban myths** has to do with alligators living in the sewers of Manhattan.*

utilitarian (yoo-tih-lih-TARE-ee-un), adjective
Designed for practical use rather than beauty; pragmatic. Characterized by a concern for the practical or useful.

*In selecting a car to buy, Hank took a **utilitarian** approach, rather than choosing the one that was flashiest or most likely to impress.*

utopian (yoo-TOH-pee-yun), adjective
Typical of an ideal world, a perfect state or place. Related to admirable but impractical ideas or ideals.

*The **utopian** dreams described in literature of the early twentieth century did not translate into realities.*

Where'd That Word Come From?

Utopian—In his 1516 book *Utopia,* Sir Thomas More invented the word "utopia" for a fictional island where everything is perfect, using the Greek for "nowhere" (*ou,* "not," and *topos,* "a place"). Eventually, this word came to mean any ideal, visionary place, and the adjective *utopian* came to describe anything that is ideal, but impractical.

utterance (UH-ter-runts), noun
Something uttered or vocalized; a word or sound spoken aloud. A style of speaking.

*How proud they were that the baby's first **utterances** sounded like "Daddy."*

vacillate (VA-suh-late), verb
To be indecisive; waver between options. To sway from side to side.

*Wishing not to **vacillate** on the issue, the mayor stood firm on his position not to raise the sales tax.*

vacuous (VA-kyoo-uss), adjective
Lacking in ideas. Having no content; empty-headed. That which is empty is vacuous.

*Some politicians are **vacuous**, telling constituents what polls reveal are the most popular positions on particular issues.*

vagary (VAY-guh-ree), noun
An unpredictable, impulsive action. A turn of events that is unexpected or capricious. Not to be confused with *vaguely*, which means not clear in meaning or intention, not clearly felt, understood, or recalled.

*The **vagaries** of the teenage mind frustrates many parents, as well as teachers.*

vanity (VA-nuh-tee), noun
Excessive pride, especially in one's appearance. Something considered futile, worthless, or empty of significance. Vanessa's vanity required her to have several mirrors in her van.

*Her **vanity** was legendary, as she could not pass a mirror without gazing into it and admiring herself.*

variance (VAY-ree-unts), noun
A difference or variation. A difference of opinion or attitude. In legal terms, the difference between two statements, documents, or steps.

*The **variance** between the positions of management and labor was so strong that a strike was inevitable.*

vehement (VEE-uh-ment), adjective
Expressed with intense feelings and conviction. Strongly felt, or marked by high emotion. Forceful and emphatic; vigorous.

In the 1960s, many expressed vehement dissatisfaction with the administration policy regarding the Vietnam conflict.

venerable (VEH-nuh-ruh-bul), adjective
Worthy of respect as a result of age, wisdom, holiness, or achievement. Dignified and worthy of admiration.

The venerable professor amazes everyone with his wisdom, sensitivity, and concern for students who are now sixty years younger than he.

verbiage (VER-bee-ij), noun
Excessive words with confusing or minimal significance. Unnecessary words or overwrought language.

Good teachers inspire students to eliminate verbiage from their writing and express themselves succinctly.

verbose (ver-BOCE), adjective
Using language that is long-winded, unnecessary, or complicated; wordy. All verbiage is verbose.

I really wanted to vote for him, because he appears intelligent, but I find his speeches are almost always verbose.

veritable (VER-ih-tuh-bull), adjective
Something that is good as true; authentic and real. Undeniably legitimate or actual. Synonymous with *verifiable*.

Granny's attic is a veritable museum of 1950s clothing, records, and memorabilia.

vernacular (ver-NAK-yoo-lur), noun
The everyday language of people as spoken in a particular country or region, in contrast to an official or formal language. The common spoken language of a group, as compared to formal written or literary language.

The vernacular of rap musicians is full of expletives and is becoming more commonly used in public places.

vex (VECKS), verb
To cause irritation. That which aggravates causes vexation.
*The constant demands of her two-year-old **vexed** Mary to the point of tears.*

vicarious (vi-KARE-ee-uss), adjective
Experienced through another person, via sympathy or imagination. To gain pleasure from actions not one's own.
*Parents often live **vicarious** lives through their children, and they do so with great pride.*

vigilant (VIH-juh-lant) adjective
Watchful and alert, especially to danger or wrongdoing.
*The family retriever was ever **vigilant** and barked whenever a stranger came near the house.*

vilify (VIH-luh-fie) verb
To make malicious and abusive statements about someone. To make someone appear as a villain.
*Even before the trial began, the accused murderer was **vilified** in the press, so the defense attorney asked for a change in venue.*

vindication (VIN-dih-KAY-shun), noun
The act of clearing someone or something from blame, guilt, suspicion, or doubt. Evidence or argument used to prove someone innocent of false charges.
*Graduating cum laude from the school that had once rejected him was **vindication** for Robert.*

virulence (VEER-yoo-lunts), noun
Rapid, extreme, and malicious, as in quick and fatal diseases. Malicious, bitter, or hostile. Not to be confused with *violence,* which means the use of physical force to injure or damage.
*The **virulence** of AIDS was shocking to physicians who did not know what was causing so many unexplained deaths.*

vis-à-vis (VIZ-ah-vee), preposition

Opposite from, or face to face with. In relation to, or in comparison to. Often misused to mean "about" or "concerning."

I would like you to discuss your raise vis-à-vis with all your supervisors and peers.

visceral (VIH-suh-rul), adjective

Instinctive, rather than based on reasoned thinking. Deeply felt; showing basic emotions. Literally "from the viscera," or bodily interior.

Not fearing any injury to herself, her visceral response was to lash out at those who threatened her children.

vitriol (VIH-tree-ahl), noun

Extreme bitterness and hatred. Writing or speech that expresses this feeling in caustic or harsh writing or speech.

How sad it is that the vitriol of all parties in the Middle Eastern conflict could not be transformed into hope.

vociferate (voh-SIH-fuh-rate), verb

To shout something out loudly; to make a noisy exclamation, demanding attention.

Susie vociferated her strong objection to her parents' insistence that she babysit for her two younger sisters.

voracious (voh-RAY-shuss), adjective

Ravenously hungry. Desiring or consuming things in great quantities. Eager or enthusiastic about an activity.

It is hoped that after you finish this English literature course you will become a voracious reader of Shakespeare.

wanton (WON-tun), adjective

Without restraint or inhibition, especially in sexual behavior. Without reason or provocation. Completely unrestrained or lacking discipline. Certainly not to be confused with *won ton*, a small Chinese dumpling.

Such wanton disrespect for the law could not be ignored or excused.

warrant (WAR-unt), verb
To authorize or guarantee. To serve as a justifiable reason to do, believe, or think something. Also, to guarantee something as the truth or dependability of something or someone.

*The child's minor accident did not really **warrant** the temper tantrum that followed it.*

watershed (WAH-ter-shed), noun
An important event, period, time, or factor that serves to distinguish two separate phases. Literally, a ridge that diverts water in a new direction.

*High school commencement is a true **watershed** event in a young person's life.*

wayward (WAY-word), adjective
Willfully disobedient. Behaving in an erratic, perverse, or unpredictable manner.

*Your **wayward** actions will someday cause you much pain, so please try to change your ways.*

wearisome (WE-ree-sum), adjective
Physically or mentally tiring or tedious. Not to be misused or confused with *worrisome*, which means causing anxiety or distress, or having a tendency to worry.

*Of course I found the 10K run **wearisome**, wouldn't you?*

Westernize (WES-tur-nize), verb
To adopt customs or beliefs common to Europe or North or South America. To impose such customs on other peoples.

*Not having visited the country in ten years, he was surprised at how much more it had become **Westernized**.*

whimsy (WIMM-zee), noun
The quality of being quaint, odd, and playfully humorous in an endearing way. An idea that has no obvious reason to exist.

*The idea of winning the lottery is for many simple **whimsy**, yet they buy a ticket each week.*

W

whitewash (WITE-wash), verb
To paint with whitewash. Also, an attempt to conceal unpleasant facts by covering them over as though they did not exist.

*How absurd his stories became whenever Brian attempted to **whitewash** his guilt.*

whodunit (hoo-DUH-nit), noun
A novel, movie, or play focusing on solving a crime, usually a murder.

*Agatha Christie's works are some of the best **whodunits** I've ever read.*

wily (WHY-lee), adjective
Skilled at using clever tricks to deceive people. The roadrunner's perpetual enemy, after all, is Wile E. Coyote.

*You shouldn't confuse "**wily**" with "intelligent," for deceiving others isn't really a smart thing to do.*

winnow (WIH-noh), verb
To separate grain from chaff by tossing it in the air or blowing air through it. To examine closely in order to separate the good from the bad, unusable, or undesirable components.

*Investigators **winnowed** through thousands of pieces to reconstruct the plan and determine factors that caused the crash.*

woebegone (WOE-buh-gone), adjective
Feeling or looking distressed or sorrowful.

*Please, Coach, go talk to the team, for they look so **woebegone** after the loss.*

wreak (REEK), verb
To inflict something violent, especially punishment or revenge. Not to be misused or confused with *reek,* which means to stink.

*It's shocking to see how much havoc a two-year-old can **wreak** in just a few minutes.*

writhe (RYTHE), verb
To make a violent twisting and rolling movement, often as a result of severe pain. To squirm with intensity.

*The running back **writhed** in agony as he waited for the trainer to arrive.*

wunderkind (VUN-dur-kund), noun
Someone who is extremely successful at a young age; prodigy. Literally, German for "wonder child."

*Little Joey was thought to be a **wunderkind** because he sang so beautifully at such an early age.*

xenophobe (ZEE-nuh-fobe), noun
Someone with an unreasonable fear or dislike of foreign people or foreign things.

*Those who express concerns about the country's liberal immigration and open border policies are regularly called **xenophobes** by those who oppose their views.*

yahoo (YA-hoo), noun
Not just an Internet portal—this words refers to an offensive, crude, or brutish person, a bumpkin.

*You shouldn't let yourself get upset by the cruel comments of **yahoos** like those guys.*

Where'd That Word Come From?

Yahoo—Yahoos, in Jonathan Swift's satire *Gulliver's Travels*, were hateful beasts in human form who prefer "nastiness and dirt." This may have been a pun by Swift on a Greek word sounding like *yahoo* that meant sleepy, or "dopey."

---

yeoman (YOE-mun) noun
An attendant, servant, or lesser official in a royal or noble household. A petty officer performing chiefly clerical duties in the U.S. Navy. An assistant or other subordinate. A loyal, dependable worker.

*All organizations need some who perform the roles of a **yeoman**, completing administrative tasks.*

young Turk (yung-terk), noun

A young person, especially one of a group, who attempts to wrest control of an organization from older, established, more conservative individuals. Historically, a member of a liberal pro-democratic Turkish nationalist movement in 1908.

How amazing it is that each of those young Turks is now worth over a million dollars after the initial public offering.

yuppie (YUH-pee), noun

A young, educated city-dwelling professional, usually regarded as materialistic and self-focused.

Do you remember when being called "yuppie" was a compliment?

Where'd That Word Come From?

Yuppie—This slang term came from the acronym YUP (for "young urban professional"). In 1983, syndicated columnist Bob Greene wrote how this word for materialistic professionals was related to an earlier word for young radicals from the 1960s: "While [Gerry Rubin] and Abbie Hoffman once led the Yippies— the Youth International Party—one social commentator has ventured that Rubin is now attempting to become the leader of the Yuppies—Young Urban Professionals."

zealous (ZEH-lus), adjective

Actively and unreservedly enthusiastic; fervent or fanatical.

At first those students named to the hall patrol seemed overly zealous, giving summonses to almost everyone.

zenith (ZEH-nith), noun

The highest point or climax of a thing or event. The peak or apex.

It's hard to predict the zenith of an athlete's career, but it is easy to identify it in hindsight.

zero tolerance (ZEE-roe TAH-luh-runts), noun
Unwavering enforcement of a rule, regulation, or law, especially regarding antisocial behavior.

*After the quarterback was caught drinking, the entire team was told that the attitude toward any future drinking would be **zero tolerance.***

zymurgy (ZIMM-ur-jee) noun
The scientific study of the brewing and distilling fermentation process. Very often the last word in any alphabetical list!

*No, I won't accept your excuse for drinking beer as a **zymurgy** experiment!*

Helpful Exercises for More Word Power and Better Test Scores

Recognizing and knowing the more than 1,000 words you should know in high school is a great first step. Now you must use the words and thus actively expand your vocabulary. This list was composed after research and communications with numerous secondary and college educators. But, as the saying goes, "The most important letter in E-D-U-C-A-T-I-O-N is *U*." What *you* do is crucial. Again and again, actions speak louder than words—at least, actions are the best amplifiers of the power of words.

The exercises that follow here can improve your vocabulary. These activities will help you focus on particular numbers of words, but if learning ten or twenty words a week is not an attainable goal, shoot for five. The quantity of words is not as important as the process involved in learning the words and the power you will gain through strengthening your vocabulary over time.

Exercise #1

1. Go back over the previous pages, and use a highlighter to identify twenty words that you find intriguing (that is, greatly interesting or curious). This might be because of their definition, because you want to try them in your next writing assignment, or because you think they are cool. Whatever your reason, create a list of twenty words you wish to know and use.

2. On a separate page, list these twenty words along with two synonyms and two antonyms for each.

3. Lastly, write a paragraph using as many of these words as possible. Make it meaningful, easy to read, and focused on a single topic. A nonsense collection of twenty words, no matter how cool or impressive, isn't what you are trying to create.

Exercise #2

Next, you can complete a dictionary exercise using ten different words from the list in this book. Although you do already have a mini-dictionary in your hands, for this exercise you'll need to use one of the heavyweight editions. Look up each of the ten words on your list, and see how it is defined. Then:

1. Look up and down the dictionary page where you found each word, and identify just one more intriguing word. For each new word, identify two synonyms and two antonyms.

2. Write a list of your new ten target words and as many of the synonyms and antonyms as you find interesting.

3. Again, write a paragraph using as many of these words as possible. Yes, make the paragraph meaningful!

Exercise #3

Choose one of your favorite magazines or newspapers. If you selected a newspaper, focus on one section that you regularly review and also on one that you rarely look at. For some, the regular section could be sports, and the other could be business, or travel and leisure. If you choose a magazine, review the entire periodical.

1. Highlight ten words in your reading that you don't recognize or cannot define.
2. Using a dictionary, or this book, look them up.

It's a good habit to look up words you don't know as you read. Don't be embarrassed. Do it!

Exercise #4

All of the more than 1,000 words in the main section of this book are good to know for improving your speaking, writing, and test-taking abilities. But about 25 percent of those words are especially good to know when you are taking a standardized test like the SAT. All of the 255 words in the next list are defined earlier in this book *and* have also been identified by several SAT preparation books as commonly used in that standardized test.

After you've read through the main word list section and done some of the exercises here, take a look at the words in this list, in groups of ten or twenty at a time. Write down your own brief definition for each, and use each one in a sentence. (Be creative!) Put a checkmark next to a word if you are not sure of its meaning.

Then go back to the main word list, and check the definitions and sentences there against your own. Pay special attention to those words you didn't remember, or where your definition doesn't match the one in this book.

After you've gone through the entire list (ten or twenty words, once a day) put it aside. Then, some weeks or months later—ideally, a few days before taking your test—take a look at the following list again. Whenever you see a word whose meaning doesn't immediately come to mind, look it up in the main section of the book.

abate	abdicate	aberration
abide	abject	abstruse
accrue	adroit	aesthetic
aggrandize	alacrity	amalgamate
ambivalent	ameliorate	anachronism
anathema	ancillary	animosity
antipathy	apocryphal	ardent
arduous	ascribe	aspersion
assiduous	augment	auspicious
avarice	axiom	bandy
barrage	beleaguer	bellicose
belligerent	bequeath	beseech
bilk	bombast	boorish
bovine	brusque	capitulate
capricious	catharsis	cavalier
chagrin	charlatan	chicanery
circumlocution	circumnavigate	circumvent
clandestine	clemency	colloquy
collusion	comely	commensurate
compunction	congenial	conjecture
conjure	construe	consummate
contravene	convivial	convoluted
copious	corroborate	covert
credence	credulous	culpable
cupidity	debilitate	deciduous
deleterious	delineate	demur
depravity	deprecate	despondent
despotism	diabolical	diatribe
dichotomy	didactic	diffident
diminutive	disconcerting	disparage
disseminate	diurnal	dogmatic
droll	ebullient	edification
effrontery	egregious	elite

elocution	eloquence	elucidate
emphatic	endemic	enervate
enmity	epicure	equanimity
erudite	esoteric	espouse
estrange	evanescent	exacerbate
exculpate	exhort	exonerate
fastidious	fatuous	fiasco
foible	fractious	garner
garrulous	goad	gregarious
guile	hackneyed	hapless
harbinger	hierarchy	hyperbole
iconoclast	idyllic	ignominious
immutable	impervious	impetuous
impugn	incendiary	incessant
incipient	incontrovertible	inculcate
indefatigable	indolent	inexorable
interpolate	inundation	invective
jingoism	juggernaut	juxtapose
laconic	laggard	lambaste
languid	lugubrious	magnanimous
malaise	matriculate	mercurial
mitigate	moribund	nemesis
neophyte	nocturnal	noxious
nuance	nullify	obesity
oblique	obsequious	obtrusive
obtuse	obviate	onerous
opaque	ostensible	ostentatious
paragon	parsimony	patrimony
paucity	pecuniary	pedestrian
pejorative	perfunctory	peripatetic
pernicious	perspicacious	pilfer
pithy	pittance	placate
plethora	polemic	pontificate

portend	prescient	pristine
profligate	propinquity	proselytize
prudent	prurient	puerile
pugnacious	quagmire	querulous
quixotic	ransack	recalcitrant
remedial	replete	reprobate
respite	restive	reticent
rhetorical	ribald	ruminate
sagacious	sanguine	scintillate
sentient	serene	skullduggery
spurious	subjugate	sublime
succinct	surreptitious	sycophant
synchronicity	tacit	tantalizing
tenable	tenacity	throng
tome	travail	trepidation
trite	ubiquitous	umbrage
unctuous	urbane	utilitarian
vacillate	vacuous	voracious
writhe	xenophobe	zenith

This exercise, and the previous three, will all pay off sooner than you think. You'll be sitting in an examination room one day—test booklet open, sharpened number-two pencils at the ready—and you'll find that a number of those difficult and obscure words found in the analogies, reading selections, and other questions are no longer so difficult, at least not for you. But that's just one of the great things that will happen when the words you should know in high school eventually turn into the words you *do* know in high school.

Appendix A

Using Roots and Prefixes to Decipher the Words You *Don't* Know

We have to admit something here. Even after reading this great book, you will still find unfamiliar words in books, magazines, newspapers, and tests.

One great way to learn new words is to break them down into smaller parts. Understanding these parts can help you make better educated guesses when trying to determine word meaning and usage. The following lists should be of value in uncovering the meaning of some of the new words that you will encounter in high school and beyond.

Positive or Intensifying Roots

am, amic (love, friend): As in *amity* (friendship) or *amicable* (friendly).

ben, bon (well, good): As in *benefactor* (person who does good), *bonus* (added rewards), or *benign* (harmless).

fid (faith, trust): As in *affidavit* (written oath).

pac (peace): As in *pacify* (to soothe), or *pacifist* (person opposing war).

sacr, sanct (sacred, holy): As in *sanctify* (make holy), *sacrosanct* (holy, most sacred), or *desecrate* (profane something sacred).

soph (wise, wisdom): As in *philosophy* (search for wisdom of life).

vit, viv (life, lively): As in *vitality* (animation and liveliness) or *vivacious* (spirited and lively).

Negative Roots

bel, bell (war): As in *belligerent* (looking for a fight) or *bellicose* (having a hostile fighting nature).

err (wander, mistake): As in *errant* (wandering, truant) or *erroneous* (full of mistakes).

fall, fals (untrue, false): As in *falsify* (lie) or *infallible* (without fault).

mal (bad): As in *malignant* (virulent), *malcontent* (someone discontented or dissatisfied), or *dismal* (gloomy, depressing).

mor, mort (death, die): As in *mortal* (something causing death), *moribund* (dying), or *morbid* (gloomy).

Other Roots

agri (field, land, farm): As in *agrarian* (having to do with farming).

anim (mind, spirit, soul): As in *animated* (full of life).

annu, enni (year): As in *annuity* (yearly pay) or *annual* (each year).

anthrop (man, mankind): As in *anthropology* (study of humans) or *misanthrope* (one who hates people).

aud, audit (hear, listen to): As in *auditory* (having to do with hearing).

auto (self): As in *automatic* (self-acting) or *automobile* (self-propelled vehicle).

brev (short, brief): As in *brevity* (briefness) or *abbreviation* (shortened word).

cap, capt, cepte, cip (take): As in *captive* (someone taken).

ced, cede, cess (yield, go): As in *concede* (to yield) or *recess* (go out).

chrom (color): As in *monochromatic* (of one color).

chrono (time): As in *chronology* (order in time).

corp (body): As in *corpulent* (fat).

dem (people): As in *democracy* (rule by the people).

gen (kind, birth, origin, race): As in *engender* (found or begin) or *generic* (universal, general characteristics).

hem (blood): As in *hematology* (study of blood).

hom, homo (man): As in *homage* (honor a man) or *homogenous* (of the same kind).

man (hand): As in *manuscript* (by hand, original) or *manipulate* (move by hand).

mob, mot, mov (move): As in *mobility* (able to move) or *remote* (far removed).

ora (speak, pray): As in *oral* (referring to speech) or *oracle* (prophet).

phon (sound): As in *phonograph* (record player).

psych (mind): As in *psychology* (study of the mind) or *psychosomatic* (between body and mind).

quer, quir, quis (ask, seek): As in *query* (question) and *inquire* (ask about).

sci (know): As in *conscious* (aware, knowing).

script (write): As in *transcript* (written copy).

urb (city): As in *urban* (of the city) or *urbane* (sophisticated and citi-fied).

vert, vers (turn): As in *avert* (turn away), or *convert* (turn from one to another).

Positive or Intensifying Prefixes

arch (chief): As in *archbishop* (a bishop of the highest rank) or *architect* (designer of buildings or the chief builder).

bene (good, well): As in *benefactor* (one who does good) or *benevolent* (wishing well).

eu (good, well, beautiful): As in *eulogize* (speak well of someone) or *euphemism* (pleasant way of saying something unpleasant).

extra (beyond, outside): As in *extraordinary* (unusual, exceptional) or *extracurricular* (outside course of studies).

hyper (above, excessively): As in *hyperbole* (overstatement).

pro (for, before, in front of): As in *proponent* (supporter) or *progress* (going forward or further).

super (over, above): As in *supernatural* (beyond the normal) and *superintendent* (one who watches over).

ultra (excessively): As in *ultraconservative* (overly conservative).

Negative Prefixes

an, a (without): As in *anarchy* (without government).

anti (against, opposite): As in *antidote* (remedy for poison) or *antipathy* (dislike, aversion).

contra (against): As in *contradict* (disagree) or *controversy* (dispute, argument).

de (down, away from): As in *debase* (lower in value) or *decant* (pour off).

dis, di, dif (not, apart): As in *discord* (lack of harmony) or *diverge* (go in different directions).

ex, e, ef (out, off, from): As in *exhale* (breathe out) or *eject* (throw out).

in, ig, il, im, ir (not): As in *incorrect* (wrong), *illegal* (against the law), or *immature* (not fully grown).

mal, male (bad, badly): As in *malediction* (curse) or *malefactor* (evil-doer).

mis (wrong, ill, not): As in *misbehave* (act badly) or *misfortune* (bad luck).

non (not): As in *nonsense* (something absurd).

ob, oc, of, op (against): As in *object* (give reasons against) or *oppose* (stand against).

sub, suc, suf, sug (under): As in *subjugate* (bring under control).

un (not): As in *untrue* (false).

Other Prefixes

ab, abs (from, away from): As in *abduct* (lead away) or *abnormal* (away from the usual).

ad, ac, af, ag, an, ap, ar, as, at (to, forward): As in *advance* (go forward) or *aggravate* (make worse).

ambi (both): As in *ambivalent* (having both emotions).

ante (before): As in *antebellum* (before the Civil War).

auto (self): As in *automobile* (vehicle moving by itself).

bi (two): As in *biennial* (every two years).

cata (down): As in *cataclysm* (upheaval) or *catastrophe* (calamity).

circum (around): As in *circumspect* (cautious, looking around).

com, co, con (with, together): As in *combine* (merge with).

di (two): As in *dichotomy* (division into parts) or *dilemma* (choice between two poor alternatives).

en, em (in, into): As in *emphasize* (put stress into).

in, il, im, ir (in, into): As in *invade* (go in like an enemy).

inter (between, among): As in *intervene* (come between).

intra, intro (within): As in *introvert* (person within himself).

meta (involving change): As in *metamorphosis* (change of shape).

mono (one): As in *monolithic* (uniform) or *monotony* (boring sameness).

multi (many): As in *multiplicity* (numerousness).

neo (new): As in *neophyte* (beginner).

pan (all, every): As in *panorama* (comprehensive view) and *panacea* (cure-all).

per (through): As in *perforate* (make holes through).

peri (around, near): As in *perimeter* (outer boundary) and *peripheral* (marginal, outer).

pre (before): As in *precede* (go before).

re (back, again): As in *respond* (answer).

se (apart): As in *segregate* (set apart).

syl, sym, syn, sys (with, together): As in *symmetry* (congruity) or *synchronous* (at the same time with).

trans (across, beyond, through): As in *transparent* (letting light through).

vice (in place of): As in *vicarious* (acting as a substitute).

Appendix B

Words of Wisdom from a High School Student, a College Admissions Officer, and a College Student

You've almost finished this book. You should now understand the power of words and why enhancing vocabulary and cultural literacy can have a positive impact on your academic, social, and personal success. You've reviewed the definitions of more than 1,000 words, and you've learned where a number of them originated.

Justin, a high school student, and Jordan, a college student, helped determine what words and phrases would be included in this book. In the sections that follow, these two young people—along with Joseph Lanning, an Assistant Director of Undergraduate Admissions at the University of Rochester—offer words to consider when seeking success in high school, during the college admissions process, while at college, and throughout the rest of your life.

Ten Words to Know for High School

Justin Nadler, having completed his junior year in high school, offers these words of wisdom:

realization (REE-uh-lie-zay-shun), noun
The act of bringing something into existence. Something that has been understood or accepted.

*I have come to the **realization** that high school is an important time, upon which I will build my future.*

Junior year is important. You realize that you are not far from college and what adults call "the rest of your life." It's not easy to look ahead when you are a teenager, because you don't want to seem too thoughtful. Yes, you do think about how many months or days are left before you get your license or before the end of school. So there are some things you want to count down, but you don't want to think too much about more school, about choosing a major, or about life after college. Realizing that you must think ahead is a bit scary, and I won't admit it to my friends, but it's something I know I have to do. Now, having helped with this book, I also realize that a good vocabulary will lead to better grades, better SAT scores, better college essays, and, if you think about it, a better future.

preparation (preh-puh-RAY-shun), noun
The work or planning involved in making something or someone ready or involved in putting something together in advance.

*High school really is **preparation** for college and more.*

Prepare yourself now for college. Start taking classes that interest you whenever possible, in addition to those you must take to meet requirements. Take elective classes that might have to do with possible college majors or careers. Even think about taking classes in the summer through special programs at local colleges or community colleges. You don't have to tell your friends you're taking them because you want to; just say your parents are making you do it. By the time you are a junior, you should begin to prepare for and think about college. Look at college Web sites, visit a few schools in person with your parents or friends, and talk to seniors about why they applied to certain schools or why they decided to attend specific schools. Don't wait until your senior year.

work ethic (WERK EH-thick), noun

A dedication to work, or a belief in the value of hard work.

Bad grades sometimes are a result of a poor **work ethic**, *not a lack of intelligence.*

High school students must start to develop, continue to build, and show others a good work ethic. Or, should I say a good *home*work ethic. Doing your homework at the same time, in the same place, and in the same way every night is a good habit to develop in high school. Good habits should never be broken; in fact, they can be strengthened when you get to college. By the time you are a junior, you should do homework because you want to, not just because your parents, teachers, or coaches say you have to. The work ethic you show on the field as an athlete, or as a club member or leader, or when you work on chores or special projects, should be as strong as your homework ethic.

independent (IN-dee-pen-dent), adjective

Free from authority, control, or domination. Able to operate or stand on one's own; not forced to rely on another person or thing.

Independent *decisions are not always easy when you are sensitive to peer pressure.*

It's about time that you begin to listen to the little voice in your head that sounds like your parents, teachers, and coaches, but it's really you. It's hard not to listen to all the voices of friends and to what you think others might say about you, but as a junior, you must begin to think for yourself. Being able to drive gives you independence from others for getting place to place. Independent feelings and responsibilities mean that you can get from high school to college with the help of others, but really through your own efforts.

confidence (KON-fuh-dents), noun

A belief or self-assurance in one's ability to succeed. A belief in someone or something to act in a trustworthy or reliable fashion.

It's hard to say which comes first, the chicken or the egg, or **confidence** *and good grades.*

Be as confident as you can, because positive attitudes can lead to positive outcomes. Coaches teach that getting psyched up can influence how you play, and that visualizing success in your mind can lead to actual success on the field. It's easy to say "Be confident" and "Don't stress about the present or future," but if you can really turn these words into feelings, you can build unstoppable momentum. Each year in school has prepared you for the next, so you should feel more and more confident as you progress. By junior year your overall confidence should be strong. If it isn't, make it stronger by working harder and finding others who will say good things about your efforts.

self-knowledge (self-NAH-ludge), noun
An understanding of oneself, particularly one's abilities, character, and motives.

It has been said that the most important knowledge that you hope to gain is self-knowledge.

By your junior year, you begin to learn who you are and what you want others to know about you. Do you like being known as a good student, an athlete, a good listener, a funny person, a good friend, or all of these? Do others know your true feelings, or are you afraid to share them? Know what you can and, when necessary, cannot do. Don't put yourself in positions to fail unless they can make you stronger. But do try to take risks if you can learn from them. Know who you are now and who you want to be in the future, and don't be afraid to let others know.

essay (EH-say), noun
A brief descriptive, interpretive, or analytical piece dealing with a particular topic; a short piece of writing assigned to a student.

The more essays you write, the better essays you write.

Essays will play a huge role in the next few years. They influence your grades in high school and also your applications to college. They also influence the grades you earn in college. Writing a good essay is very important, and by the time you are a senior, you should know how to do it. But you can always improve your writing skills. Believe me: If I can help write a book, then anyone can write great essays.

assistance (a-SIS-tunts), noun
Something done for or given to provide aid to or assist someone else.

Don't ever be afraid to ask for assistance.

People are ready to help you. Parents, teachers, tutors, and friends can help with academics, sports, and personal issues. Asking for help is a sign of strength and maturity, not a weakness. High school students should be mature enough to ask for help without being embarrassed. They know what's at stake if they don't and how much can be gained if they do. Also, seniors can help juniors and others in lower grades. Sometimes the best way to earn good grades is by helping others with classes you find easy.

options (OP-shuns), noun
Choices, possibilities; the range of available decisions that one faces.
   Be open to explore colleges, universities, community colleges, and other options after graduation.
   Don't be afraid to explore everything, even if it may seem an unusual or embarrassing subject to discuss with friends. Examine things like post-grad years at private schools and internship programs. At first be open to many things, and then share those that are most interesting. Last, take steps to reach your goals and ask for the help of parents, counselors, brothers and sisters, teammates, and coaches. You can't do it alone.

commencement (kuh-MENTS-munt), noun
The act of beginning or starting. Also, a ceremony for conferring degrees or granting diplomas at the end of an academic year.
   Your commencement ceremony marks both an end and a beginning.
   While some call it "graduation," others call it "commencement." It means the beginning of the rest of your life, not just the end of high school. Learn from the past, and look forward to the future. It is a little bit scary, but it is your future and it will be great.

Ten Words to Know When Applying to Colleges

Joseph Lanning is an Assistant Director of Undergraduate Admissions at the University of Rochester. He offers the following ten words and phrases that every high school student who is applying to college should understand and think about.

#1: Interview

If a college offers this option, take it. It is hard to make yourself look bad, and it shows your interest in the school, as well as your ability to communicate. It is the opportunity for you to develop a meaningful one-on-one relationship with an admissions counselor or alum who will share his or her evaluation with the admissions office. This kind of personal exchange usually only enhances your candidacy, so it is not something to be feared or avoided.

#2: Research University

A *research university* is one where the faculty both creates and teaches knowledge; at other schools, often smaller ones, the faculty is more focused on teaching the knowledge that others have created. While no one type of institution is always better, one may be better for you. The resources, tone, and style of each type of school are all different. Find out what options one will give you over the other. If you can, talk to faculty and ask what courses they teach, particularly if they teach freshmen and sophomores and why they like teaching these courses. Ask if they do research and whether they involve undergraduates as research assistants, not just subjects. See if the school you are exploring encourages undergrads to conduct original research, if you can support the research of faculty and doctoral students, or whether these opportunities exist at all. Most high school students are not familiar with the amazing impact that research can have on one's academic experience, so you have to ask questions and learn about this facet of higher education prior to deciding where to apply and where to attend.

#3: Curriculum

Educated consumers of any product need to look deeper. You cannot tell a book by its cover, but you can tell a college or university by its curriculum. Every college and university has dorms, classrooms, teachers, dining halls, security, and libraries. But not every school has academic requirements. What now makes institutions distinct is largely how much you define class selection or how much a set of predetermined courses defines this process. You need to know how much freedom of choice you want or need and how much a school offers. What would be the requirements of a particular school? What is their curriculum and the purposes of this approach? How soon can you start taking courses you are truly curious about? What happens before you declare a major, and after? Ask these questions and think about the answers as you determine your hit-list of schools and, ultimately, the admissions offer you accept.

#4: Admissions Counselor

This person is a college's first line of defense and offense. This two-way player actively recruits large numbers of applicants, yet screens and admits only the few that meet specific profile characteristics. He or she is the person who makes the final decision to keep your application in the admit pile and sometimes has a role in how much aid and scholarship you get. Whenever and wherever you get to meet them, they assess and track your interest and serve as a resource to answer questions and address specific issues. As a recruiter, this person appropriately promotes a school. As a counselor, he or she should be ready and willing to help you navigate the sometimes-confusing process of college admissions. An admissions counselor can explain who reads an application, if it is read more than once, and how scholarships are allocated.

The admissions process varies from school to school, so knowing a counselor at each institution you apply to is invaluable. Don't let the fact that a person might also serve to evaluate or rate you scare you away from getting to know this valuable resource professional. The second word in this title—"counselor"—should be the most important one.

#5: Diversity

Diversity in the student body involves religion, political preference, gender, sexuality, geographic and socioeconomic background—the list is truly endless. Visit schools to see the amazing variation of people and backgrounds you will be living and studying with for four years. Talk to students about their views and how diversity positively influences their lives. Also, examine an institution's diversity in programs and majors. Are there many options to choose from? How much choice do you truly have when choosing courses, overseas studies programs, internship options, majors, and more? Diversity truly has many definitions and many meanings on a college campus. What does this word mean to you, and why?

#6: Financial Aid

Here is one important distinction to know. *Merit-based* aid is based on specific academic or achievement-focused criteria, while *need-based* aid is offered based upon the financial status of the student and his or her family. For each school you are interested in, ask the following questions. What are the criteria for scholarships, grants, and loans? Do scholarships affect how much additional aid you get based on your financial needs? What do you have to pay back, and what is a grant? What additional paperwork (FAFSA/CSS Profile) is needed to be eligible for aid? These questions and the answers you receive are critical as you progress through the admissions and, ultimately, the decision-making process. Ask these and many, many other questions. Don't be shy, and do talk to your parents about these issues. Together, the more you learn, the more you know, the better your decisions will be.

#7: Wait List

A *wait list* is a pool of students who barely missed the criteria used for admissions. These are highly successful and motivated students who for one reason or another just missed the first so-called "cut." If you find yourself on a wait list, be sure to express your interest in a school by providing additional information and supplemental documents. You can do this through another visit, a formal letter, a brief essay, or a phone call and follow-up e-mail. It is a time to prove that you really want to be at *this* school and that you won't settle for anything less. It's not a time to be passive and wait for the next letter from the admissions office.

#8: Rankings

Those rankings of schools that you see in various publications may be important to some applicants and not for others. They can be confusing if not examined carefully. Above all, they should not be the sole criterion used when determining where to apply and where to enroll. Please make an effort to examine and understand how rankings are created, the criteria used, and which of these factors may (or may not) be important to you. Certain things—like "selectivity" (numbers of applicants versus number of offers), "peer reputation" (how other schools perceive an institution), or "alumni giving rate" (the percentage of alums who donate)—may not be of interest to you personally, though they may be of interest to another applicant. Do be careful when using rankings.

#9: Alumni Involvement

The level to which alums become involved and contribute to the continued growth of their alma mater is a subjective indicator of what a school offers undergraduates. This is a difficult thing to quantify, so you must depend upon quality interactions with alums to make good decisions. Make an effort to meet alums from your short list of schools. While at first they might be interviewing you, after you have received an offer of admissions *you* should be interviewing *them*. Seeing the products of a place, uncovering their recollections, and learning about how they stay involved in making the place better can be strong indicators for how happy you would be at a school yourself. Interact with young alumni and not-so-young alumni. Each group will have an interesting perspective and, ultimately, the information they share will help you make your choice regarding the school that in four short years you may call "my alma mater."

#10: Fit

How comfortable you feel at a college is the most important part of the decision-making process and possibly the most difficult to define. By visiting the campuses of the schools you are interested in, perhaps staying overnight, you can best determine fit. The fit of a school is like the fit of a shoe. If you buy it because it looks nice, but you don't try it on first, you could be very uncomfortable later. And, size, style, and purpose do matter. Get to know the community the school is in (rural, urban, or suburban), the nature of the area, and, more important, what students do on campus and off. Talk to ordinary students, not just the tour guides. Ask whether they feel the school fits them or why they fit the institution. You have to be comfortable to learn to your maximum potential.

Ten Words to Know in College

Jordan Nadler, our college-student coauthor, reflects upon ten words or phrases that high school students should know about being a college student.

change (CHAYNJ), noun
Alteration, variation, or modification (important rhyming words) or the results of these. A variance from a routine or pattern, most often a welcomed one.

Change is scary but necessary as one grows.

College brings big change, and not just to your address. Your whole world changes, from academics to friends, food, sleep patterns, study habits, and social life. Realize from the beginning just how much change you will have to face. Welcome change as natural to diminish anxiety, and it will make the transition easier. Change is good!

advisor (ad-VIE-zur), noun
Someone who gives advice. Someone who advises students on academic issues, including course selection.

College advisors are always crucial, yet the best ones are not always those officially assigned the job.

When you walk into a class, don't just consider whether a professor or subject matter will be interesting. Think about whether this person would make a good formal or informal advisor. In college, your advisor is your strongest advocate, your source of advice, and your friend—or can be, if you choose well. At some schools, you have a general advisor or a group of general advisors available until you declare your major. After that, you are either assigned or you select someone from within your chosen academic department to serve as your "major advisor." But please, don't limit those who serve as advisors to persons who hold specific titles. Everyone can and should be thought of as an advisor and advocate. The sooner you identify a faculty member, administrator, or older peer who can be an active listener and inspirational counselor, the sooner you can start building a relationship that can truly help your college career.

independence (in-duh-PEN-dunts), noun
Freedom from dependence on or control by another.

Independence at college is a blessing, a curse, and ultimately a gift to be used wisely.

In his list of words, Justin mentioned that high school students need to work to become more independent. College offers growth potential and independence like you have never had before. Embrace it and use it for good. Just because your parents aren't around doesn't mean you should go crazy. Well, it's almost as simple as that. Establish good habits on your own. Learning how to be independent, how to schedule time well, will only help you have more fun, less stress, and fonder memories as college progresses.

For me, independence means identifying daily and weekly to-do lists or goals and then scheduling time to complete them. Knowing what I have to do, and when, helps me stay on track and, frankly, independent. If assignments and readings take control of you because you have ignored them, then you are clearly not very independent. If you maintain control over them, then you are the master of your academic, social, athletic, and personal schedule. And you can get some sleep in as well.

choice (CHOYSE), noun
The power or chance to choose among different things; the decision to select one thing, person, or course of action over another.

The choices between one class and another, one teacher or another, or one major and another are just some of those that you can expect at college.

Classes, professors, living arrangements, going to the game, dinner, sleep? Should I cram for that exam, or have I studied enough? What major and why? College offers so many, many choices. While at times you feel that you have to make these choices alone, in truth you always have someone to turn to if you need advice. So don't rush into important academic or life-altering decisions, but don't fret over them either. Seek feedback from friends, family, faculty, and professional advisors when needed. Don't sweat the small stuff, and always think about consequences, especially when you are deciding whether you've studied enough and if it is time for a little fun. Do take advantage of the great opportunities college has to offer. It is a once-in-a-lifetime scenario. Learn how and when to make serious choices and when to be spontaneous and intuitive.

add/drop (ad-drop), adjective
Referring to the practice of allowing one to change one's original selection of academic courses by adding or removing courses after the beginning of the semester.

*During the **add/drop** period you have the time to decide which courses are really right for you.*

Thank goodness that many decisions, including those about course selection, are not permanent. That's one of the beauties of college. Don't be afraid to sign up for a class or two that may be out of the norm. In fact, when you want to carry a load of five classes, do sign up for six, or if you want to finally narrow down to four, you can start with five or six. Even as a first-semester freshman (although many don't realize it), you can shop for and try on classes to see if they fit. Attend classes for a week or two to see if they fit your schedule, your academic areas of interest, or your long-term goals. If you hate the class, or there are scheduling conflicts, or if you are not in the mood to write the five required papers, you can always drop it, as long as you do so before your school's add/drop deadline. In fact, these two words, or one "slashed word," may be among the most important and practical for you to know.

flexibility (flek-suh-BIH-luh-tee), noun
The ability to change or be changed according to circumstances; the capacity to be influenced, or persuaded to change.

*Success often follows **flexibility**, specifically in situations involving a variety of tasks.*

The oxymoronic "planned chaos" of a college day can bring unexpected challenges, and frustrations, so be ready to compromise. Whether altering your study habits, rethinking the appropriateness of a Halloween costume, or freezing when it starts to snow in September (if you decide to go to school in upstate New York), be ready for all that college throws at you, and take it in stride. While you are on your own, you are rarely alone, and you must learn to flex with circumstances and with people in order to minimize stress and conflict.

time management (time MA-nidge-ment), noun
The process of deciding how to divide the amount of time available among various tasks and activities.

*Once you are living on your own, good **time management** is an essential skill.*

For most students there are no required or supervised study halls in college, and no teachers, coaches, or parents will hound you to do your homework or show up for practice or class. College in most circumstances offers the structure of scheduled classes, but few other chronological requirements are part of any given day. You need to make your own daily and weekly schedule and stick to it. Find ways to put your schedule on paper, in a spreadsheet, or a PDA. Keep your schedule handy, regularly update it, and reward yourself when you stay on target. Personal rewards, whether a latté, some TV, DVD, or CD time, or an IM to friends, reinforce positive time-management behaviors. The stuff that adults and other books tell you is true. Time management is the key to college success.

experience (EK-spear-ee-uhns), noun
Involvement in an activity, or exposure to events or people, leading to an increase in knowledge and skills. Knowledge of and skills gained by being involved in or exposed to something over time.

*Do maximize the quantity and quality of **experiences** you have in college.*

Where else can you give blood at lunchtime, and then play inner-tube water polo; learn about the ocean floor before breakfast, then go back to bed; or, after a very busy day, go to a hockey game and party until tomorrow? College is a unique blend of eclectic experiences. Don't be afraid to try new things! And, as that old saying goes, "Learn from experience, for it is the best teacher."

home (HOME), noun
Where a person or family lives together. The place where a person finds refuge, security, and safety, where they can receive rest, nourishment, and shelter.

Home for some is thought to be where one's heart is, but for all it is where both one's head and heart are.

College isn't just a place where you study. It is that proverbial home away from home. For approximately four years, it is where you sleep, socialize, dine on the finest cuisine (just kidding!), and learn by reading, listening, and questioning. The sooner you make college your home, the better. Once you feel secure in this setting, success follows in all areas of this new life. But never forget that you can have two or more homes; two places where the people you love share space, and where you can feel safe and nurtured. Yes, home is where your heart and head are. It's an attitude and not just a place. Look for it, and you will find it wherever you go.

fun (PHUHN), noun
A feeling or an activity that provides a time of enjoyment or amusement.
*It's strange, but some think it's **fun** to be in the library when it closes.*

Don't forget to have fun! With the stress of the known, of midterms, papers, and finals, and the unknown, of the future, you can lose sight of the fact that college is fun! Well, it is! So go out and have some!

These are the words that I hope will help you realize what college is about. I've only been out of high school for a few years, but I encourage you to make the most of your time there. Build a strong foundation for the four years after high school (college), and beyond (life in the real world). The words that make up your written and verbal vocabulary are really the brick and mortar upon which the exciting edifices (a great word, that one) of your life will be constructed and constantly renovated. Words do create worlds— literary, social, academic, and career worlds. Use them to create the best places for you and those you love.

About the Authors

Burt Nadler has been an Assistant Dean of the College and Director of the Career Center at University of Rochester since 1998. Within these roles he has been actively involved in the university's admissions efforts and other areas of student life. He regularly reviews and edits documents that greatly impact students in their quest for success, including resumes, cover letters, and graduate school personal statements.

Justin Nadler is a member of the Pittsford Mendon (New York) High School Class of 2005. He is a proud member of the Pittsford Lacrosse Team, as a midfielder. Justin has successfully faced many academic challenges with determination, and he has used many resources including tutorial services and supplementary study guides. His academic strengths include sports marketing, art, and Spanish.

Jordan Nadler is a member of Cornell University's Class of 2005. She has studied at the University of London's School of African Studies, and she has completed the University of Dreams and the Washington Center for Internships programs. At Cornell, she is a dual major in Near Eastern studies and government who has earned dean's list recognition for all academic semesters. With her father, Burt, Jordan coauthored *The Adams College Admissions Essay Handbook,* sharing with her peers many of the lessons she has learned as a college applicant and an admissions essay writer.

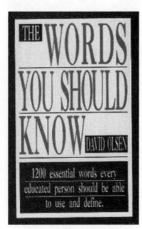

Also Available:

MORE WORDS YOU SHOULD KNOW

1500 More Words Every Educated Person Should Be Able to Use and Define

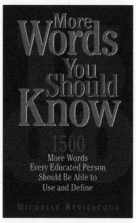

Trade Paperback
ISBN: 1-59337-236-1
$9.95

A companion to our previous title *The Words You Should Know*, *More Words You Should Know* contains 1,500 additional words that every educated professional should understand and use with ease. This book saves you time by condensing the daunting amount of words included in dictionaries into an easy-to-read format. It's the most complete work of its kind—and that's no hyperbole, rigmarole, or embellishment!